AMERICA'S CHANCE *for* SURVIVAL

(WHAT I BELIEVE)

ISBN-10: 1461095387
EAN-13: 9781461095385

AMERICA'S CHANCE *for* SURVIVAL

(WHAT I BELIEVE)

⟱⟱⟱

HANK SIMS

A book is not read on a shelf
If it was worth reading, pass it on!

To my wife, Linda, who said
"It looks like you are writing a book"

THE AUTHOR'S THESIS:

Everyone is biased. One cannot believe anything just because someone says it. Sometimes someone says something that is true, but one has to be astute enough to recognize that it is true.

When you recognize that some things are left out of history books and that you begin to doubt what scientists say; when you hear politicians state numbers as facts while other politicians use different numbers to describe the same event; you must begin to wonder what to believe. You begin to wonder what the information is that is used in making decisions and laws that impact all of us. If you distrust the information you ingest, how can you trust what you yourself believe.

I want you to question what you hear when deciding what you believe.

I hope that by the next election, my writing will have made you think and possibly become more humble in determining what it is that *you* believe.

Call me Old Fashioned; I'll take it as a compliment.

I feel my effort is just a compilation of the thoughts of others, with an analysis of what I can believe considering the various thoughts. What I believe has been changed during the writing of this book.

As I know what I believe has changed during the writing of this book, I hope that the reading of it will make you think about what *you* believe.

I know that no one will agree with all of my thoughts. I, like everyone, am a unique individual. I fear that few if any of my thoughts reflect actions by our government. I believe that movements of government, in the direction of some of my thoughts would be movements in the right direction.

I hope that I may cause a Liberal to think about what he believes, and why.

If I quote Ronald Reagan more than other presidents it is not necessarily that I think he was our greatest president (George Washington was) but some of his quotes are the best. He said, "Before we spend more money doing what we are doing, we should first determine if what we're doing is part of the problem." He also said "Government isn't the solution to our problem, it is the problem."

He was the "Great Communicator."

CREDITS

I want to thank those who contributed to my writing this book. Firstly, my wife. She said she thought that I must be writing a book. I wasn't yet but then I got serious about it. The "History Group" at Grace Covenant Presbyterian Church in Williamsburg, Virginia is a professed conservative group focusing on the study of history. They contributed ideas and their "history" programs added material for my book. My brother, Lester, contributed his experiences in the Holy Land. Also, I want to recognize the input of Glenn Beck. He didn't know it but he added content to my book; on his recommendation, I read ATLAS SHRUGGED. I also want to thank Chad Sims and Kelly Fisher for their additions. The biggest contributors were ABC, CBS, NBC and FOX News programs. What they do and don't report, and more importantly, how they report about the world and Washington, D.C. influenced me greatly. I also want to thank Mary Fisher and Larry Gentry for their encouraging words.

TABLE OF CONTENTS

ANNEXES

FOREWORD

It was as this country began struggling with what was to become the Great Recession of 2009 that I became acutely aware of politics, economics and the direction of our country. My fears for our country began to crystallize. After hearing repeated polls that asked, "Are you are pleased with the direction the country is going?" with increasingly negative results, I began studying the situation.

While my opinions are continuing to be updated by further study, my conclusion is that this country has peaked. I believe the USA quality of life for all citizens has peaked. I believe the Great Recession of 2009 was the bell ringer. The peak had already passed but nobody noticed. The big crisis will occur when interest rates increase from their current, historic, lows. The interest on the federal debt will overwhelm the budget.

OUR COUNTRY HAS PEAKED

I believe we should be concerned about the survival of our country instead of the marginal benefits of universal health care, unemployment benefits, government subsidies and political correctness and that we should become the humanitarian nation that many of us think we are.

I have tried to say what I believe and describe some areas where the country must change.

In order to survive as a country, I believe we must begin with the following actions:

1) Follow the constitution or amend it.
2) Reduce spending and repay the National Debt.
3) Revise the tax code and eliminate taxes on things we want to encourage.
4) Change our priorities.

We should return to limited government and free market economy.

CHAPTER I

REASONS FOR MY CONCERN

My reasons for concern are described below. There is nothing new. Political cartoons have described these items; comedians past, notably Will Rogers, and numerous comedians later made light of our government. Ayn Rand wrote *ATLAS SHRUGGED* 50 years ago describing the likely outcome.

There is nothing new but something *must* be done before these actions lead to the history-indicated final result.

Politics. Congress has lost contact with the people. Greed is rampant. Too many politicians work for their own benefit instead of working to represent their constituents. They make deals to benefit their individual states, their major contributors, special interests, or themselves (unconstitutional; Article IV, Section 2). These deals are frequently called "Earmarks" or "Pork." Any such deal is for the benefit of few, at the expense of the whole (the taxpayer), which they are supposed to represent. Government spending rewards inactivity and wasteful consumerism.

Spending is totally out of control. Congressional spending exceeds the tax base so that borrowing money to support the spending has become the norm. This is irresponsible and is in fact a Ponzi scheme. Bernie Madoff is in prison for a similar activity.

Discussion

Many congressmen (42% in the 212th Congress) are lawyers by profession. They will rarely if ever pass laws that infringe upon the incomes of themselves or other lawyers. This applies equally to amendments to the constitution. Legislators are the only ones empowered to amend the constitution, and the needed amendments are not in the self interest of legislators.

SELF INTEREST IS GOOD FOR CAPITALISTS NOT FOR LEGISLATORS

I fear that self interest is a driving force behind most congressmen. They strive for the good of their state (earmarks), or for a certain group of people (the poor; the unions, etc) or for the good of their major contributors. However, the real reason for these efforts is to ensure their re-election.

"A POLITICIAN THINKS OF THE NEXT ELECTION, A STATESMAN OF THE NEXT GENERATION"
James Freeman Clarke

The people who want something for nothing will continue to elect the same government, because that government will continue to support the people who get something for nothing. Unfortunately, the people getting benefits directly from the government are in the majority. Sixty percent of households get more from the government than they contribute (USA Today, Apr 6, 2010).

I believe the USA is a republic; it is not a democracy. Sub-elements of the definition of republic are Aristocracy, Oligarchy and Democracy. I believe we fit the definition of Oligarchy because the professional politicians have accomplished the deception of the people to the effect that incumbents are predominately re-elected. This allows them to be an Aristocracy, or by definition the country is an Oligarchy. The constitution says that the "United States shall guarantee to every State in this Union a *Republican* form of Government", Article IV, Section 4. The constitution does not use the word democracy.

> "Washington is every bit as unaccountable
> to the people as the British Crown was."
> TAKING BACK AMERICA by Joseph Farah, p 185.

The election in November 2010 showed a decisive vote for smaller government and reduced spending. It resulted in electing many Republicans. But since that time the 2012 budget has been proposed as a substantial increase over the last year's record budget. The house is discussing ways to save tens of billions from a budget that is increased by hundreds of billions to the record $3.7 trillion budget. They didn't get the message!

I believe that it is neither the Democrats that are at fault, nor the Republicans. It was the Bush administration that approved the Troubled Asset Relief Program (TARP) with a $700,000,000,000 cost. This got Obama elected. Now Obama has continued with Cash for Clunkers and rebates for purchasing energy efficient appliances and assistance to home purchasers. They bought GM. The 2011 budget is so large that it hasn't been yet approved by the first of April, 2011, six months and counting, after it was due; we continue with weekly extensions so as to not default. The continuing increases in the budget resulted in the large Republican victories in November 2010. Doesn't anybody get the message?

THE GOVERNMENT HAS LOST TOUCH WITH THE PEOPLE

President Obama is not responsible for the crash in home values that contributed so much to the Great Recession. I believe the problems were begun by President Carter and exacerbated by each following administration.

*It is the **system** that is broken.* The career politicians are far too often re-elected based on charisma rather than issues. It is this, ignorance on the part of the voters, and the congressional Quagmire, discussed later, that is at fault. *Major change* is needed.

Unconstitutional actions: The founding fathers were not ignorant. They were well read in the history of the Enlightenment period in Europe. They were aware of the problems in Europe, that's why we had the Revolution. They wrote the constitution in the best way they could to give us a government for the people and by the people.

They gave specific powers to the federal government and left the other powers to the states. The educational system, medical insurance, medical research, subsidies to universities and companies for research and even production, abortion, gay rights, etc were not powers given to the federal government; therefore, all federal actions in these areas (and many more) are unconstitutional. Many of these items are not even governmental issues.

The constitution is a simple document, it has 7885 *words*. It is easy to read and understand. I find it hard to understand how it can be misunderstood so frequently by our leaders.

DNA is a recent scientific development. Interestingly, convicted felons have been tested for DNA analysis of the evidence used to convict them; many have been proven innocent.

I believe we should have a similar analysis of existing laws and decisions to see if they follow the constitution. Remove those that do not!

> "OUR CONSTITUTION PROTECTS
> ALIENS, DRUNKS AND
> U. S. SENATORS"
> Will Rogers

Unconstitutional actions include, but are not limited to:

By the Judicial branch:

Legislating from the bench; that is, making decisions that are not based either on written law or on the constitution. Numerous violations of the 6th Amendment.

By the Executive branch:

Legislating by choosing whether or not to enforce laws written by Congress (Article II, Section 3); Specific current issues are immigration laws; laws against slander and libel and entering into un-declared wars.

By Congress:

Usurping Judicial and Executive prerogatives by controlling the budget and by legislating and budgeting for unconstitutional activities; Obamacare, The Voting Rights Act of 1965, etc. Buy funding National Public Radio (Amendment I.)

By all Branches:

Endeavoring in areas excluded from their powers. Usurping the Rights of the States.

Discussion

Judicial Branch:

Brown versus the Board of Education is a classic example of the misuse of the constitution. While the decision may have resulted in a proper action, it was for the wrong reason. The policy of separate but equal is NOT unconstitutional. It is not addressed by the constitution unless it is "a power reserved to the states or to the people." If this decision were to be properly made, it would be made by Congress by enacting a new law.

I was quite disturbed when I heard that the Supreme Court had decided in favor of the demonstrators in the Westboro Baptist case. They decided that people have a first amendment right to demonstrate in front of a solemn funeral of an American veteran. Amazing! I guess it was a proper decision, though morally degrading. I believe the problem is in the judicial system that allowed it to get to the Supreme Court to be tried on the basis of free speech. I believe the demonstrators should have been arrested and potentially jailed for disturbing the peace. If they didn't disturb the peace or violate any other decency law, I have to agree that they had a right to do what they did, at least in this world. Why did this case get to the Supreme Court?

I was surprised to hear that the Supreme Court decided a case that said one cannot sue a drug manufacturer for a faulty drug. I was confused when I heard the next day that a suit was proceeding against Tylenol. What is the law, and if the courts can decide in this manner, how is a citizen to know what is right; what he can legally do? How did this case get to the Supreme Court?

How did these cases that should have been decided in state courts get to the Supreme Court while multiple cases to repeal Obamacare have not?

<u>Legislative Branch</u>:

Laws favoring one state over another (earmarks/pork) are prohibited (Article IV Section2).

Finalizing the tax code in December of the tax year is an ex-post facto law prohibited by the Article I, Section 2 of the constitution.

"Nowhere in the enumerated powers of Congress is there authority to tax and spend for Social Security, government schools, farm subsidies, bank bailouts,

> food stamps, creating official 'art,', disaster relief, national police forces, and other activities that represent roughly two-thirds of the federal budget. 'Neither is there authority for congress' mandates to the states and people about how they may use their land, the speed at which they can drive, whether a library has wheelchair ramps and gallons of water used per toilet flush', writes Williams, 'A list of congressional violations of the letter and spirit of the constitution is virtually without end.'" Joseph Farah TAKING AMERICA BACK, p 210

Passing Obamacare with obviously un-constitutional elements. The Constitution does not allow for the government to force the people to buy a product. If that is not constitutional, the whole law cannot be constitutional. How can one element of the law be arbitrarily taken out of a law without knowing how it impacts the rest of the law?

I believe 38 governors have filed suit to be exempted from the law. Hundreds of waivers have been granted.

WAIVE A LAW?

Further, the law has been found to have imbedded in it a budgetary commitment and tax increase that usurps the congressional duty to fund governmental activities.

Executive Branch:

The Department of Justice is noted as being selective about which laws it chooses to enforce. The classic case is the lack of enforcement of federal immigration laws in Arizona. Their actions to prevent Arizona from making and enforcing their own immigration laws are not only unconstitutional; the actions are wrong and reprehensible.

> The Department of Justice is now in the process of suing a school. The school had denied leave for a Muslim teacher. She had applied for leave for a pilgrimage to Mecca, in accordance with her religious beliefs. Once in a lifetime a Muslim should take a pilgrimage to Mecca, if able. The teacher had been working for the school for nine months and wanted three weeks' leave. Her leave request was denied resulting in the DOJ suit. Fox News, March 29, 2011 asked "Or [is the] Justice Department out of control?"

In February 2011, President Obama determined that the 1996 Defense of Marriage Law that bars federal recognition of same-sex marriages was unconstitutional and directed the Department of Justice to stop enforcing the law. Attorney general Holder said a crucial portion of the law was unconstitutional. What is wrong with this action? In my view;

The president was right in specifying that it was only federal recognition that he could bar. The issue is not mentioned in the constitution as a specified action, therefore it was... left to the states. Therefore any action by the federal government is inappropriate. And, *if* it were a constitutional issue, it should be determined by the Supreme Court, not the President.

President Obama's determination that he should not enforce this law is unconstitutional. Article 2 section

3 says that the president will take care that the laws be faithfully executed. It is the President's job to enforce laws, Congress makes the laws.

Attorney General Holder's consideration that a crucial portion of the law was unconstitutional making the whole law unconstitutional is similar to the Obamacare requirement that everyone buy health insurance. If a portion of one law being unconstitutional makes the whole law unconstitutional, a portion of another law should make that law unconstitutional.

President Obama in one action abrogated his responsibility to enforce laws and usurped both Congress' and the Supreme Court's responsibilities to make and interpret laws.

In March 2011, U. S. forces took military action in Libya under the presidents order, to prevent unnecessary civilian deaths in the suppression of a rebellion (a humanitarian mission?) In May 2011 the president had not yet gotten congressional authorization for that war effort.

The constitution requires a declaration of war to be approved by the Senate. All wars since WWII have been "police actions", not requiring a declaration of war. The constitution, Article 1, section 8 states; "*Congress* shall have the power ...to declare war...."

James Madison said the word "'make' war was changed to 'declare' war in the constitution to allow the Executive the power to repel sudden attacks but not to commence war without explicit approval of Congress." (Note that he said "Allow the Executive the power to repel *sudden attacks*"; he did not say to "extend influence.")

The War Powers Resolution of 1973, Public Law 93-148, provides that the President can send U.S. Armed forces into action abroad only by authorization of Congress or if the United States is already under attack or serious threat. It forbids armed forces from remaining for more than 60 days without...authorization...or a declaration of war.

Did George Bush overstep his authority by passing the Patriot Act?

It is essential that the President not step beyond his powers as established by the Constitution.   The Constitution; Article II, Section 3, states that "— (The President) shall take Care that the Laws be faithfully executed. It is the presidents job to enforce the law, not to make the law nor interpret it, those are the roles of Congress and the Supreme Court.

Aren't unconstitutional actions impeachable offenses? Is the President (Congress?) above the law? I know that there *MUST BE* later laws that justify our police actions, but how far away from constitutional principles must we veer before we wake up and insist that our leaders get us back on a lawful, constitutional track?

Is there no mechanism to ensure that all branches of government adhere to the constitution?

Legal Adjudication. I recently read that there was an assassination attempt on FDR in Feb 16, 1933. The perpetrator was executed on Jan 30, 1934. Imagine how long the trial would have taken today and how many lawyers would have been involved; how much the cost of litigation and imprisonment would be. The country is being strangled by legal adjudication.

The perpetrators of the 9/11 attacks on the World Trade Center on 9/11/2001 have not been tried yet!

Punitive Damages are prohibited by Amendment VIII.

Lengthy trials are prohibited by Amendment VI.

Class action suits should be prohibited since they usually solicit citizens to sue where they otherwise would not; and they are normally seeking punitive damages. Instituting frivolous lawsuits should be a crime.

Advertising by lawyers should be limited as it was until recently.

Political Quagmire. Congress has grown beyond its ability to function. To function, it has organized into a political party structure and manages by committee and sub-committee. There are so many Representatives that they cannot hope to know each other or have a meaningful discussion. Today there are 435 Representatives. In 1790 there were 3.9 million Americans or about 130 representatives. The founding fathers could not have conceived of having 435. The senate has 100 members vice the original 26.

> "The more you read and observe about this Politics thing, you got to admit that each party is worse than the other."
> —Will Rogers

Who is the "Democratic Leadership in Congress?" Large government is not representative government. It is so large that it spends all its time managing and deceiving itself.

The large number of congressmen results in unnecessary, in fact, counter-productive expenditures for their staffs and in the numbers of lobbyists employed to influence them. They are forced to spend vast amounts of time, and thereby, money, to organize their actions in order to get anything done. They choose to organize by party affiliation, which exacerbates the difficulties of coordination and polarizes the process.

Interestingly, both houses of Congress have chosen to be seated when in session, by party affiliation to further limit effective communication.

The committee and sub-committee system establishes "pockets of knowledge" and incomprehensible laws. Congressmen vote on bills that they cannot possibly have read or understood. News broadcasts regularly describe congressional discussions where one "side" doesn't believe what is said by the other; inconsistencies are highlighted. Surely our forefathers did not imagine that lawmakers could have become so removed from the facts that their actions would be cursory, mistaken, immoral or unconstitutional.

IS THE COUNTRY'S BIGGEST PROBLEM TOO MANY CONGRESSMEN?

The net impact is that the party structure operates largely by "block" vote. The number of issues decided by a vote "along party lines" is astounding. Congressmen have party caucuses. They apparently decide how they will all vote on specific issues. It seems that none can think or vote individually.

It appears that there are only two effective Senators and two Representatives; one Republican and one Democrat.

Political Maneuvering and deal making:

The media frequently discusses communications between and among congressmen and the deals that are made. A congressman will support a certain bill if another congressman will support another. It appears that a substantial amount of congressmen's time is spent negotiating what "earmark" or"pork" should be funded. Congressmen are graded based on what federal funding is provided their state. They must get something for their state to get *re-elected.*

I heard one citizen state that he would not vote for re-election of a Senator: "She hasn't done anything for the state." She had not achieved any earmarks that brought federal money into the state.

I guess the epitome of political maneuvering and deal making is the Obamacare legislation:

In an address to Congress in 2009, the President said, "No federal dollars will be used to fund abortions." But the House bill would permit a "public option" to cover all abortions, and federal subsidies are to be used to purchase private insurance that covers abortions.

"No federal dollars will be used
To fund abortions."
Barack Obama

The president repeated his promise that his plan won't add "one dime" to the federal deficit. But legislation offered so far would add hundreds of billions of dollars to the deficit over the next decade, according to the Congressional Budget Office.

In his speech, the president said he would reduce the price tag, saying "the plan I'm proposing will cost around $900 billion over 10 years. That's about $100 billion less than what the CBO said the House bill would cost."

He also said there will be a provision in this plan that "requires us to come forward with more spending cuts if the savings we promised don't materialize."

The Ulsterman report stated that to repeal Obamacare would save $1.3 Trillion; "CBO comments indicate $540 Billion savings over 10 years if Obamacare is repealed."

President Obama's own debt commission said the alleged savings to come from Obamacare is a gross exaggeration. Despite the administration's claim that Obamacare would save $180 billion over 10 years, the commission described such savings as "phantom savings".

WHAT DO YOU BELIEVE OF
WHAT YOU HEAR?

Former House Speaker Nancy Pelosi was quoted to say that we must pass the Obamacare law so that we can determine what is in it. The bill had some 395,000 words, how long would it take to read and understand it? Other bills are likewise presented for vote with insufficient time for a congressman to read them before the vote.

Why are bills and government policies so long, so wordy? Is it in order to employ more writers? Is it to satisfy lobbyists? Lengthy documents take a long time to write. They take a long time to read. Sometimes understanding is impossible. But these documents are the guidance for governing our country. The Constitution has 7885 *words!*

Congressional votes in enacting this law were almost exclusively along party lines. I am sure that none understood it, and I doubt if any even read it in its entirety.

What was the information used as a basis to pass the law?

Obamacare became law in 2010. By April 2011, hundreds of waivers had been granted. I read, on-line, the Louisiana letter to the U.S. Department of Health and Human Services requesting a waiver. I guess the constitutional duty of the President to "take Care that the Laws be faithfully executed," (Article II, Section 3) above means "unless waived."

Representative Weiner (D, NY) was a strong, even vehement backer of the Obamacare Bill. However, on March 24, 2011, he was on the news asking for a waiver for all or part of the Obamacare Law for the city of New York. I thought federal laws applied equally to all Americans.

Nancy Pelosi's district in northern California has received one of the greatest numbers of waivers.

On the same date, I heard that the Andy Griffith advertisement in support of the Obamacare Bill cost the government (taxpayer) $3,600,000. Now, when did the government start buying advertisement from the Media (Amendment I); I thought that was what News programming was for. Worst yet, how did the funding get approved when it was not yet determined which side of the issue Congress was on?

The bill has now been law for almost a year. Does anyone know what's in the law or what it will cost or save?

Following closely behind Obamacare in illustrating political Quagmire is the effort to pass the 2011 federal budget.

The 211th Congress did not pass the bill, awaiting the 212th. It appeared the 211th congress did not want their actions on the 2011 budget to be reflected in the November 2010 elections. The 211th congress passed a continuing resolution.

The 212th Congress is now made up of a Republican majority in the House and a Democratic majority in the Senate. The Republicans feel the November 2010 elections gave a mandate to reduce federal spending; reduce the budget. But the Democratic Senate would not agree and there was the threat of President Obama's potential veto of a reduced budget is a threat.

Congress approved at least six additional continuing resolutions to avoid "closing down" the government.

WHAT IS THE DEFINITION
OF QUAGMIRE?

In February 2011 Congress went on vacation one week before a stopgap budget was required to prevent government shutdown or default. This was after a Democratic Senate would not approve a House sponsored budget. Of course, the Republican House of Representatives would not compromise.

Continuing debate over the House proposed $80B cut in the 2011 Presidents budget has led to repeated threats to "shut down" the government. No matter which "side" prevails, it is proof positive that the leadership is not concerned about the Survival of America. They are concerned only about looking good by blaming the "other side". They want to safeguard their political careers.

LEADERSHIP IS NOT CONCERNED ABOUT THE SURVIVAL OF AMERICA

The latest reason the Democratic Senate held was that the republican house initiative did not include funding for "Planned Parenthood", the biggest provider for abortion in America. Note the President's address, earlier, where he said "No federal dollars will be used to fund abortions."

On April 8, 2011, one hour before the deadline, there was apparent agreement; the government would not be shut down. The $80B cut was reduced to $38.5 and funding for Planned Parenthood was not cut.

FEDERAL FUNDS CONTINUE TO PAY FOR ABORTIONS

On March 27, 2010, President Obama appointed Dr. D. M. Berwick as Director of Medicare and Medicaid. Congress was not in session so the required Senate confirmation could be bypassed.

In the same timeframe, in Wisconsin, the Democratic component of the Senate deserted the Senate. They went to Illinois for the purpose of preventing the Republican majority in the Senate from passing any legislation; a required quorum could not be made without the missing Democrats.

Are these cases political maneuvering or just plain Dirty Politics? Where is responsible government?

"Read my Lips."

"The era of big government is over."

"I did not have sexual relations with that woman."

I believe our government has become so convoluted that no one knows what's happening. Congressmen don't read bills they approve, they don't agree on estimates or impacts. They do not know what to believe. *If Congressmen do not know what's happening, how can they govern?*

Is there a vision for the country? Who should or could write it?

DO CONGRESSMEN KNOW WHAT'S HAPPENING?

Is it possible both at federal and state levels to come to a deadlock so that nothing can be done? There ought to be a law. There ought to be some moral backbone in our leaders.

There is a lot of discussion about budgets and budget cuts. People use numbers in arguing for their position. Sarah Palin stated that entitlement programs will consume the entire federal budget by 2035. Another person says Social Security will be solvent until 2030. Budget expenses or cuts are normally projected over 10- year periods.

Do they think they even know what the world will look like in 2035? Why waste time projecting things that cannot possibly be predicted accurately?

> "THE STUPIDITY OF OUR LEADERS AND
> POLITICIANS IS UNBELIEVABLE."
> Donald Trump, 3/21/2011

President Jimmy Carter tried to pass a Zero Based Budget. He realized that there was room for cost reductions at all levels of all departments (some might call it fluff). The bureaucracy defeated him; it simply did not work. He wanted to know what he got for what he spent. All the departments could *or would* tell him was how much they were spending and that they needed that much to continue what they were doing. If he asked them to do something different; they would always want more funding. If they were ever backed to the wall to reduce their budget, they would offer up a program for cancellation. This would be their most essential program. I observed some of these actions first hand.

> FIRE THE BUREAUCRAT
> THAT CAN'T TAKE A CUT.

Congressmen are citizens. They should live under the same laws as citizens. Congressmen should contribute to and receive Social Security or they should contribute to their own retirement program with potential employer matching funds like most businesses. They should receive retirement benefits only as earned by time on the job, like everyone else.

Lawmakers should be liable to the same laws as other citizens; egs, sexual harassment, libel, slander, etc. If candidates were subject to libel and slander laws, they might speak more about their own plans rather than defaming their opponent when campaigning. I don't want to limit free speech but do want to prevent half truths and lies by candidates.

Candidates tend to cater to the low political IQ of the voter and to denigrate their opponents rather than campaign on relevant issues. Candidates are elected based on charisma and popularity rather on ability or issues.

Legislators should not be treated as an Aristocracy with excessive pay and unusual benefits. All laws should apply equally to all citizens. Politicians should be representatives of the people, not be representatives of their own careers.

> "NO PERSON IS ABOVE THE LAW,
> NOT EVEN THE PRESIDENT."
> Newt Gingrich

A recent news commentary indicated that "civility" is going out of politics; brutal personal attacks and negative campaigning seem to be the rule. I see outright lying by candidates. The media frequently interviews a congressman regarding what he has said. The congressman sometimes says that it was "taken out of context" or maybe even that he "misspoke." Interpret that; he lied!

CONGRESSMEN SHOULD ABIDE BY
THE LAWS THEY PASS
OR
ARE THEY ABOVE THE LAW?

Political campaign financing should be limited. Expenditures on elections have skyrocketed. Phenomenal amounts are spent. The impact is to ensure that only the elite have a chance to be elected. Massive contributions by special interests are required for a candidate to have a chance. The political impact of this is obvious and sad. The tax code revision, discussed later, would reduce the tax advantage of contributions by special interests.
Speaking time should be limited. Was there ever a benefit of a filibuster, or is it just another attempt to achieve minority rule?

> "However [political parties] may now and then answer popular ends, they are likely in the course of time and things, to become potent engines, by which cunning, ambitious, and unprincipled men will be enabled to subvert the power of the people and to usurp for themselves the reins of government, destroying afterwards the very engines which have lifted them to unjust dominion." Geo. Washington 1796.

The Vote:

The right to vote is not covered in the Constitution unless it is, "reserved to the states." (Amendment X)

ONLY FREE WHITE MEN WITH PROPERTY CAN VOTE

"There is no right to vote in the United States Constitution, so each state's standards have evolved separately unless federal laws were passed that applied to every state. When this country was founded, only white men *with property* were routinely permitted to vote (although freed African Americans could vote in four states). White working men, almost all women, and all other people of color were denied the franchise.

By the time of the Civil War, most white men were allowed to vote, whether or not they owned property, thanks to the efforts of those who championed the cause of frontiersmen and white immigrants (who had to wait 14 years for citizenship and the right to vote, in some cases). *Literacy tests*, poll taxes, and even religious tests were used in various places, and most white women, people of color, and Native Americans still could not vote." Cobb Lamarche, 2004.

The Constitution does not address voting. Decisions as to who can vote were left to the states. Various constraints to voting were imposed by the states including, among other things, poll taxes and poll tests.

The 14th amendment removed voting from state sovereignty and ensured the vote to all male citizens being 21 years of age.

The 15th amendment removed race, color or previous servitude as reasons to deny the right to vote.

The 19th amendment extended the vote to women.

The 24th amendment prohibited a poll tax.

The Voting Rights Act of 1965 (42 USC 1973-973aa-6) outlawed "discriminatory voting practices...Prohibits states from imposing... *literacy tests...* that prevented African-Americans from exercising the vote."

Today, the wording of the Act should be considered an insult to African Americans.

THE CONSTITUTION CANNOT BE CHANGED BY PASSING A LAW— IT REQUIRES AN AMENDMENT.

I personally believe the Voting Rights Act of 1965 is unconstitutional. It changes the constitution; a law is insufficient. There should have been a Constitutional Amendment. I also believe the founding fathers did not intend that non-contributing members of society should vote.

How can democracy survive with voters ignorant of government and issues? A test is needed.

All one has to do to know of the lack of knowledge of issues of is to listen to interviews of "the man on the street." The uninformed sometimes give totally erroneous answers to important questions. It is often astounding, yet these people vote.

On February 25, 2011, Fox news cited a poll saying 48% of Americans think Obamacare has been repealed, based on publicity of actions in the House of Representatives. The senate had not acted on the issue let alone the president. How clear can it be that our population is not an informed population?

An election official when meeting a resident that she knew had not voted asked her why she had not voted. The response was, "I didn't vote because nobody came out and told me who to vote for." Shocking, but true.

"NOBODY TOLD ME WHO TO VOTE FOR."

I fear this is a major motivation of the "Get out the Vote" campaigns associated with elections. Politicians know that people who they "get out" are likely to vote as they suggest. While this is not technically buying votes, the morality of such efforts is questionable. Major political parties and other respectable agencies wanting to sway the vote to their own interests participate in these efforts.

WE SHOULD TAKE A TEST TO VOTE

Newsweek, March 28, 2011 had an article titled "How Dumb Are We?" "Newsweek gave 1000 Americans the U.S. Citizenship Test. 38% failed. *The country's future is imperiled by our ignorance.*"

In talking with an acquaintance about politics, he said. "We believe that driving is a right but we are required to take a test before we are allowed to drive. Voting is really a more important right than driving, why aren't we required to take a test to be allowed to vote?"

CHAPTER II
HISTORICAL PERSPECTIVE/PHILOSOPHY

Prosperity: My theory is that prosperity is not sustainable. Current news about low birth rates of Europeans (indeed all developed nations); the immigration Moslems in Europe and the immigration of Mexicans in America (both groups having relatively higher birth rates); and other related news lead me to that conclusion.

PROSPERITY IS NOT SUSTAINABLE

Prosperous people hire others to serve them. Prosperous people have smaller families, having no need for the labor of their children and also so that they can ensure prosperity for themselves and their children. We claim, as a right, a high standard of living/luxury. We import hard working Mexicans to do our work; Europeans import Turks, Pakistanis, Indonesians, etc.

The immigrants work for less and fill the low paying jobs while our government pays us a minimum wage or welfare to ensure our high standard of living. (People depending solely on welfare have a high standard of living compared most of the world's population or our own earlier generations (e.g., the "Greatest Generation")).

We are already seeing the Mexican/Moslem impact in our vote. They want more: health care, welfare, public housing, even public education that the government can give them by transferring wealth from the more prosperous.

Typically, Mexicans and Moslems do not limit their family size, so that over time, there is a proportional increase in their numbers. The prosperous become fewer in proportion to the workers and the poor. The big wheel turns and the prosperous start realizing a problem. But, by now the workers/poor are in the majority and are ruling or will be after a climactic event (civil war? Or governmental collapse through sinking in national debt). Then comes a big famine, a dark age, until someone again becomes prosperous enough to hire or enslave someone and begin gaining wealth. The cycle repeats.

It's a theory. I believe it is a cycle that cannot be reversed. It is consistent with Rome. Other historic civilizations have suffered the same fate and many current states are showing the symptoms. Please enumerate the governments in the world that have survived for 200 years. However, supporting this theory:

Philosophers:

Plato (600 BC) wrote that phase one of a society was the *production* phase where people work and produce individually to better themselves and their families and therefore their society. Then 2) they begin to become a *service society* where they hire or subscript or enslave to get their production done to enable them to live and hopefully prosper. 3) The *investment phase* where they invest in others' plans for production to obtain what they need to live and prosper. Then finally, 4) which comes just before the *inevitable* downfall is the *gambling phase,* where there is little production for workers to invest in; so they wager against one another in an attempt to maintain their life style. Of course, in the last phase there is little growth; so the size of the pool of goods keeps shrinking until the society collapses by evolution, revolution or invasion by someone willing to produce (the Roman collapse?).

At about the time our original 13 states adopted their new constitution, in the year 1787; Alexander Tyler (a Scottish history professor at The University of Edinborough) had this to say about The Fall of the Athenian Republic some 2,000 years prior: "A democracy cannot exist as a permanent form of government. It can only exist until the voters discover that they *can vote themselves money from the public treasury.* From that moment on the majority always votes for the candidates promising the most money from the public treasury, with the result that a democracy *always* collapses over loose fiscal policy followed by a dictatorship. The average age of the world's great civilizations has been two hundred years. These nations have progressed through the following sequence: from *bondage* to *spiritual faith,* from spiritual faith to *great courage,* from courage to *liberty,* from liberty to *abundance,* from abundance to *selfishness,* from selfishness to *complacency* from complacency to *apathy,* from apathy to *dependency,* from dependency back to *bondage."*

ARE WE IN THE SELFISHNESS, COMPLACENCY, OR DEPENDENCY STAGE?

"Instead of the 'Compassionate Conservatism' that George Bush promised in his 2000 campaign, what has characterized the ideological core of today's GOP is Absolutism, not Conservatism. There is the Absolutism of the free market, and ideology of no taxes, no regulations, no safety net—indeed, no government beyond what's required to protect private property and provide for the National Defense.

There's the religious absolutism of the Christian Right, a movement that gained traction on the undeniably difficult issue of abortion, but which soon flowered into something much broader; a movement that insists not only that Christianity is America's dominant faith, but that a particular, fundamentalist brand of that faith should drive public policy—", Barack Obama, THE AUDACITY OF HOPE, p 46 describing the GOP policies that *he wanted to defeat.*

"In country after developed country, the fertility rate fell below replacement level. In the late 1900's in Europe, it fell to 1.4." (Vice 2.1 replacement level), National Geographic, January 2011 p 48.
Proposed Constitutional Amendment; "Congress shall make no law abridging the freedom of Production and Trade", Ayn Rand, ATLAS SHRUGGED, p1168.

Thoughts of the Founding Fathers. Many of the Thoughts of the Founding Fathers are reflected in the Declaration of Independence and Constitution and Bill of Rights. Other quotes from our Founding Fathers reflect on our country's definition. These thoughts reflect their understanding that ours is a new way of government. They show the concerns of the Founding Fathers about the *long range survival* of our way of life, of our liberty and our Country.

They also reveal ways in which we have deviated.

Quotes of Thomas Jefferson:

"The democracy will cease to exist when you take away from those who are willing to work and give to those who are not."

"I am not a friend to a very energetic government. It is always oppressive."

He also said that a democracy requires an informed population.

A DEMOCRACY REQUIRES AN INFORMED POPULATION

Quotes of James Madison:

"A popular government without popular information or the means of acquiring it is but a prolog to a farce or a tragedy, or perhaps both."

"A well-instructed people, alone, can be permanently a free people."

"Each generation should be made to bear the burden of its own wars, instead of carrying them on, at the expense of other generations."

Quote of Samuel Adams:

"A general dissolution of Principles and Manners will more surely overthrow the Liberties of America than the whole force of the Common Enemy."

Quote of John Adams:

"Remember democracy never lasts long. It soon wastes, exhausts, and murders itself. There never was a democracy yet that did not commit suicide." —John Adams, letter to John Taylor, 1814.

DEMOCRACIES COMMIT SUICIDE

The Wealthiest Generation. The current generation is, by far, the wealthiest generation of our history.

> My sister eloped when she married. Both of my brothers eloped also. I, the youngest, had a Church wedding. My wedding was in the church where I was a member, therefore at no cost. I paid the preacher a $25 honorarium. We had probably 30 relatives attend. My cousin invited us to her house after the wedding. I guess we might now call it a reception. Someone baked a cake, I don't know who. It was great. We've now been married 42 years.

My two daughters married. Their weddings cost about $7,000 each with some 100 guests.

At dinner, after church one Sunday, we discussed the trend. I asked if anyone knew *anyone* under 40 who had an economical wedding. There was general laughter.

The "Greatest Generation" defined by Tom Brocaw, is the generation that fought WWII. They fought for their homeland. They fought to preserve prosperity for their posterity. Most of them did not have indoor plumbing; many had no electricity.

That generation left a huge inheritance for their descendents.

The current, Wealthiest Generation capitalized on this inheritance; they spent it. In order to sustain the wealth when times began to get difficult, they borrowed from later generations, to ensure the current level of prosperity.

We should be ashamed!

CHAPTER III

CHRISTIAN BASIS OF OUR COUNTRY

Basis.

The Christian basis of our country is supported by certain evidence:

The Declaration of Independence, paragraph 2, "We hold these truths to be self-evident, that all men are created equal, that they are endowed *by their creator* with certain unalienable Rights----.

"The highest glory of the American Revolution was this: it connected in one indisolvable bond the principles of civil government with the principles of Christianity," John Quincy Adams.

Thomas Jefferson is quoted as saying, "Indeed I tremble for my country when I reflect that God is just, that his justice cannot sleep forever."

The Ten Commandments are proudly displayed on the facade of the Supreme Court and in numerous State Capitol buildings and other public places.

The Mayflower Compact describes that their journey was taken "For the glory of God and advancement of the Christian Faith" among other factors.

The U. S. Calendar has eleven national holidays. Other holidays vary slightly by state. Two of these holidays, Christmas and New Year 's Day are Christian holidays (New Year 's Day celebrates the first day of the New Year in the *Christian* calendar). Sunday is the first day of the week and not a work day for most Americans. Why are there no Jewish, Muslim, ..., Buddhist holidays on the U.S. calendar?

Sunday is the first day of the week and is still observed by many Americans as "A day of Rest."

"In God we Trust" remains on all U.S. currency.

However:

In 1962, the Supreme Court decided that Prayer in schools is unconstitutional. (A blatantly unconstitutional action).

Easter Break was celebrated by most schools until that was recently renamed "Spring Break."

The Department of Justice, the ACLU and congress are continuing to place limits on expressions of Christianity. Will we have to remove crosses from our national cemeteries and remove religious artwork on public buildings?

Are their motives truly anti-religious or simply politically correct?

Actions persist to force removal of roadside crosses marking the sites of traffic deaths.

I heard a recitation of the Pledge of Allegiance on 3/2/11 on Fox news. The recitation left out the phrase, "Under God". It was done in a politically correct interpretation.

Separation of Church and State does not mean Suppression of Church by State! I think I invented that saying.

Islamic Impact.

My brother wrote "When we went to Israel last year our bus driver was a Muslim and he informed us that the Muslims did not have to conduct war on Israel in order to subdue them. They only had to be patient because their average family size was 4 children and Jewish was less than 2 children. His explanation was that Muslims were devout and most Israelis were Atheists and that Atheists had no reason to have children since children interfered with their current standard of living; and if you have no religious reason to continue your lineage, most will simply live for the current highest standard of self indulgence. Unfortunately many so-called Christians have this same mindset.

Otherwise, I would call Islam as a political force a Theocracy, much as Communism, National Socialism or Fascism were Theocracies, demanding worship of the state—same was true in Egypt, Greece, Rome. The difference is that Islam dictates worshiping Muslim teachings vs. worshiping the state. They are all totalitarian and believe that use of force is justified to provide social benefit and to obtain moral and spiritual control. When Christian mottos are not allowed in public buildings we are getting close—which is the scary thing!" End of my brother's input.

I have a concern that the current Moslem actions are simply a continuation of Mohammad's original plan. His plan was to conquer the world. That conquest began in the seventh century. Significant milestones in this war are 632, 691, 732, 846, 1096-1229, 1244, 1453, 1492, 1700, 1801-1805, 1906, 1919, 2001 and 2009. Our current situation is just a continuation of the previous events.

Mohammad was born in the 6th century. He died in 632. At the time of his death, Islam had spread throughout much of the Middle East and northern Africa.

The Dome of the Rock was built 688-691 on the Temple Mount, a Christian holy site in Jerusalem.

Muslim Moors invaded Spain and Portugal. In 732 Battle at the battle of Tours, Charles Martel defeated the Muslim Moors as they invaded France from Spain.

In 846 the Muslims attacked Rome but made no lasting conquest.

From 1096 to 1229 Christian Europe conducted five Crusades to re-conquer the Christian Holy land. These Crusades contributed greatly to the romantic history of Medieval Europe. Success was variable, with re-conquests of Jerusalem, and treaties but the Muslims re-took Jerusalem in 1244. The Christian holy lands remained in Muslim hands until WW I broke the Ottoman Empire.

1453 marked the fall of Constantinople, and Moslem expansion into Europe was released.

The Moors were expelled from Spain by King Ferdinand and Queen Isabella in the same year that Columbus discovered America, 1492.

In 1700, the Turks laid siege to Vienna Austria marking the high-water mark of their advance into Europe until the twentieth century.

Virtually from the end of the American Revolution, Barbary Pirates roamed the Mediterranean Sea capturing ships and enslaving their crews. After various negotiations and several payments of tribute by the U.S., a war resulted. From 1801 to 1805 a war persisted. Final resolution was not achieved until 1815.

In 1906, we were at war with the Philippines. The U.S massacred numerous Moslem Moors, The Imperial Cruise, Chapter IV.

In September, 2001, Muslim terrorists struck down the twin towers of the World Trade Center, in New York. The action is remembered simply as 9/11.

In January, 2009, twelve were killed and thirty wounded at Ft. Hood Texas. A Muslim officer was the shooter.

This sequence of events reminds me of the 100 Years' War between France and England. The 100 Years' War was not a continuous war but a series of battles or wars stemming from a continued hostility. Is this a 1400 years' Muslim/Christian war?

THE 1400 YEARS' WAR

"WHILE EUROPE SLEPT, by Bruce Bawer is; a clarion call for the west to understand the Radical threat to our Freedoms from Politicized Fundamentalist Islam." Andrew Sullivan. Pages 51-55, relate the progress of Muslim immigration into Norway.

He writes that at first, Norwegians described Muslims as *enriching*, just as many Americans describe their children's multi-cultural education as "enriching."

He says that the Muslims were later viewed as *needy victims* and the Norwegians as heroic benefactors. It appears consistent with the American experience of both Mexicans and Muslims, who now often qualify for American welfare, food stamps, low income housing support. They often get federal assistance to pay for a college education, even though many are in this country illegally.

Next, Norwegians were told that they *must adapt* to the ways of their new countrymen. I know it is a controversy as to whether Muslims can be governed by their own Sharia Law or abide by the laws of the host nation, e.g., Norwegian, Dutch, French or American. This becomes a real issue when one realizes the substantial difference between Sharia Law and the laws of their host country. Examples are arranged marriages and honor killings, etc. Are we adapting when signs in most stores are in Spanish?

As Muslim residency matured in Norway (I don't know about citizenship?) Mr. Bawer relayed that Muslims were responsible for 65% of the rapes in that country. *Under Sharia Law* the responsibility for the rapes, in many cases, lay with the woman. Norwegian women dress provocatively soliciting sex (or rape) and the man should not be held accountable.

AMERICANS ARE ADAPTING TO MUSLIM WAYS

I guess we in America are in the "must adapt" phase of Muslim immigration. Plans for a Moslem Mosque near "ground zero" are progressing over opposition that stresses that it could be perceived as a *monument to 9/11.*

Europe News, 29 March 2011 said that in 2008 European Union members were instructed they must "Condemn and combat Islamophobia" and to "ensure that school *textbooks* do not portray Islam as a hostile or threatening religion". However, German Chancellor Angela Merkel recently said "Multiculturalism has proved an absolute failure," The *Christian counter-offensive has begun.*

Our current news, March 2011, is reporting a 13-year-old American girl who ran away from home to avoid a marriage in Pakistan arranged by her Muslim Step-Father. I haven't heard yet of a high percentage of rapes being attributed to Muslims in this country.

There are strong indicators that there will be another war, a religious war. It will be Moslem vs. Christian. Reasons are that the Koran encourages killing non-believers and the fact that the Moslem birthrate exceeds that of Christians. Muslim immigration into Europe and America has made Muslims a substantial minority. Sharia Law is followed in many areas.

When the Moslem population gets to be sufficient, there *will* be war unless Christians willingly yield.

As I read it, Nostradamus predicted WWIII as a western alliance against a Muslim alliance. Both Nostradamus and the Mayan Calendar predict a date in December 2012.

My wife made an interesting statement; "Just as Edison said necessity is the mother of invention, Desperation is the Mother of Revolution." I really don't know anyone else to attribute this quote to.

Islam is already at war with the U.S. They have repeatedly stated it. They call us the great Satan and call for killing all infidels (us). George Bush responded to the *Moslem Terrorist Act* at the World Trade Center on September 11, 2001. He said "we are *at war with terrorists*", (he did not say Moslem). However, I have searched and cannot find any recent instance of Christian terrorism in the U.S.

> Fox News, March 25, 2011:   "Thousands of Christians displaced in Ethiopia after Muslim Extremists torch Churches, Homes". "On November 9, Christians in Breskeno, Kenya woke up to find notes on their doors warning them to convert to Islam, leave the city or face death";

War with Christians is in their religion, in the Koran. The 12th IMAM says Mohammad will return and rule for seven years; the world will be cleared of the infidel (includes Christians) and the world ends. The Koran also says that it is the right and duty of the faithful to plunder and enslave those who do not acknowledge the prophet. We are at war but we just don't know it yet.

WE ARE AT WAR BUT
WE JUST DON'T KNOW IT YET

I personally don't advocate drastic measures. I don't seek inhumanity but I believe we should recognize that there is a religious problem. Indicators are that we must take actions to alleviate the situation before it is too late. We should not ignore the problem because it is simply not politically correct. If we recognize the problem in time that we can deal from a position of strength, we may be able to get a negotiated and enduring peace. We must enforce our National Laws now.

Separation of Church and State does not mean usurping of Church by State any more than it means usurping of State by Church.

CHAPTER IV
TAX STRUCTURE

Our current tax code has been developed over many years. Progressive or regressive taxation is a political issue. What is allowed as deductions is a political issue. The relative taxes on commodities and activities are political issues. It is time to clear the tax code of archaic contents, to simplify it, and reduce its negative impacts on our economy and limit the numerous politically motivated changes.

Discussion

Taxes. Recognize that the tax code influences where monies are spent. Consider that we want to encourage industry, employment, savings, investment, industry, trade, home ownership. Why do we tax all of these things and thereby discourage their existence? Why do we subsidize things we want to discourage?

Reduced taxes on each item that we want to encourage will spur growth in that area. Specifically reducing business/industry taxes at all levels would reduce the cost of goods we buy. It would also reduce the cost of our exports—encouraging an improved balance of trade. Most importantly, it would reduce the exporting of jobs and contributing to unemployment among Americans.

Eliminating these taxes would certainly spur growth.

"...We tax our companies at higher levels than the Europeans tax theirs. In fact, 2009 marks the twelfth year in a row in which U.S. rates have been higher than those in the rest of the Organizations for Economic Cooperation and Development (OECD)." THE BATTLE, A. C. Brooks, p 85

STOP EXPORTING
JOBS

We are currently *subsidizing* imported oil, the thing we *most* want to discourage.

We are currently subsidizing petroleum products to ensure the lowest possible "price at the pump." Since "Alternative Energy" programs are not cost effective, we are also subsidizing them so that they can be sold to compete with oil. Why not just burn the money?

Why not tax imported gasoline (oil) sufficiently that alternative energy becomes cost effective instead of subsidizing both of these programs?

This increased gas tax, which could be a tariff, would obviate the need for arbitrary fuel efficiency rules for automakers and the need for government enforcement; the market place would do that. An increased tariff on oil would reduce the importation of oil and encourage use of more economical cars.

We could, and I believe should, use tariffs in lieu of taxes to both discourage importing oil and make alternative energies cost effective, when possible, without subsidy.

WE COULD INCREASE THE TAX (TARIFF) ON OIL AND HAVE NO INCREASE IN OUR OVERALL TAXES.

The appropriate increase in the tariff on oil and reduced government subsidies of both petroleum and alternative energy, if done judiciously, with a decrease in income tax, could have a net tax cost of zero.

Increased taxes on all other imported items (tariffs) would also increase tax revenue and reduce the export-ing of jobs. While this is desirable, it must be balanced with the related restrictions on free trade. (Note that this is constitutional.)

If these tax adjustments are not sufficient for govern-ment operations, the balance should be taken by either a national sales tax (preferred) or a flat rate income tax.

Deductions. Deductions allowed by the current Income tax structure are a tremendously political issue. Most of the deductions have, in my view, undesirable impacts some of which are discussed below.

Deductions of political contributions encourage the excessive cost of elections and often purchase influence that, in turn, is reflected in the tax code.

Marriage related deductions contribute to the Gay Rights activism. While I don't believe it is the government's business to say that gay people should not enter into contracts equivalent to marriage, and with the same financial considerations, I do not believe it is the government's right to destroy the sanctity of Christian Marriage. That violates the separation of church and state.

Charity deductions necessitate bookkeeping and encourage lying. A gift is a gift and should be given without anticipation of reimbursement. Charitable gifts should not be a mechanism for avoiding paying taxes.

Tax credits, rebates, grants and subsidies. In most cases one of these terms refers to a benefit given to one person at the expense of others (taxpayers), a transfer of wealth. They also interrupt the utility of capitalism and benefits of competition.

INCOME DISTRIBUTION
TAXPAYER TO SPECIAL INTEREST

We are currently subsidizing alternative energy sufficiently that it can compete on a cost basis with oil. However, we are subsidizing oil so that the price at the pump is lower. We are spending money to encourage importing oil and we are spending money to discourage importing oil. But it is worse than that. By using ethanol, the demand for corn is increased. That increases the cost of corn used to produce food that we eat and food that livestock eats.

It increases the cost of groceries and meats. Another, hidden, tax! It also degrades the balance of trade.

Likewise, I understand that we are subsidizing programs for "Planned Parenthood" and for "Save the Children;" programs with contradictive objectives. Why not just burn some more money?

GOVERNMENT DOESN'T HAVE AN INCOME PROBLEM, IT HAS A SPENDING PROBLEM

The tax rebate in 2009 (Cash for clunkers) for purchasing new, economical cars rewarded people who had been wasteful in buying non-economical cars. People who had already been frugal were penalized. Additionally, this penalized the most needy since only the wealthier segment of society was able to afford to buy the new car even with the rebate. The process also took off the market a large number of the cheaper autos that the poorer citizens may have desired.

Income Tax Preparation: Under current laws preparation of the income tax forms by individuals and businesses is a gargantuan task. It employs numerous professionals in the business of assisting in this process. It employs another whole department of the government, the IRS, to check behind the tax preparers and citizens and businesses.

As mentioned above, the tax code is a political issue. Politics determine tax rates and who gets what deductions or credits. The resulting tax code is rather complex. It is hard to understand and it changes continuously, sometimes after the fact, as mentioned above.

I have to believe the tax code is often unfair. I know it encourages cheating. Why else would there be an IRS to check behind all of us?

> "The Income Tax has made
> More liars out of the
> American people than golf has."
> Will Rogers

I have reached another conclusion. I believe that expenses involved in preparing taxes and auditing taxes produce nothing but the preparation of taxes. The IRS recognizes the complexity of the code and recommends that you have an accountant or tax advisor assist you. This results in more non-productive effort and expense. There is no net benefit to society. The tax code needs revision.

I would like to describe some of my personal experiences with income taxes.

Firstly, my parents, not college educated, always took their taxes to town for someone in the bank to calculate.

But I was arrogant. I am college educated with an advanced degree. I feel I should be smart enough to figure out how to fill out a 1040 form. Maybe I didn't realize one has to study the code continuously to keep up with the changes, virtually a full time job. I did my taxes myself anyway.

The taxes code is complex; it requires much bookkeeping and careful reading of the tax brochures (before Turbo Tax). There were two important dates in life; December 25 and April 15. I anticipated one and dreaded the other. I normally began working in November to meet the April 15 date.

In the early 1980's there was income tax averaging.

I bought a vacation cottage; used it some and rented it some. When it came to doing taxes, I depreciated the house. In fact, I could get more tax back if I used "accelerated depreciation", so I did. After some five years, the house had appreciated in value. But, my kids were entering the college years and my expenses skyrocketed. I decided I could not realistically keep the house so I sold the house.

I started to do the taxes that year. When I looked for the form for income averaging, I could not find it. Then, I learned the tax code had changed. I couldn't spread my gains over five years like I had planned; I had to pay taxes on the total in the current year. The depreciation of the house claimed in previous years, under a different law became a "profit." It put me in a much higher tax bracket.

I did not keep my tax records for 25 years past so I cannot give a number. But I lost almost all of my capital gains to taxes. I think I began to realize part of the purpose of the tax code is to ensure income for income-tax professionals.

I felt cheated; still do.

Last year, I sold another house. In this "Great Recession", I just couldn't afford two homes. Anticipating the tax loss I would claim for losses sustained in the sale, I sold several stocks in which I had profits. I wanted to sell the stocks in 2010 and use the loss on the house to offset my gains on the stock. I anticipated, if I sold in another year, I would not have the tax loss as an offset.

> "We have tens of thousands of federal laws, rules, and regulations that no one can understand. No one could possibly have the time to read them— not even the lawyers who have to specialize in particular fields just to be proficient. So what's the point? The point is to set traps...." TAKING BACK AMERICA, by Joseph Farah, P 33

In doing my taxes, Turbo Tax documented my sales value, expenses, etc and calculated my loss, some $18,000. It then gave a warning 'A loss on a house is not a deductible expense'. I was shocked. Once again I had failed to keep up to date on the changing tax laws. My logic was simple; if you have to pay taxes on a gain, a loss is deductible. Another major financial loss. I should have employed a tax professional.

I felt cheated again!

In further researching this issue, after the fact, I found other references to my tax problem:

"IT'S A HOMEOWNER'S worst nightmare: Selling your home at a loss. Sadly, many folks have discovered just how devastating this can be." Smart Money, March 20 2011.

"Will the IRS let you claim a write-off for the loss? Nope. You can only claim a tax loss on investment property. A loss on a personal residence is considered to be a nondeductible personal expense for federal income tax purposes. Most states follow the same principle. Double ouch!" Smart Money, March 12, 2011.

Citing IRS advice, The Washington Post, July, 14, 2007 said "You should have an accountant or tax adviser assist you in calculating the loss."

Just what I needed. Other people come upon the same surprises and the government advises more support for the tax manipulation industry, because the tax structure is too complex for most citizens to understand.

I would expect that many readers can supply similar stories.

ALL EFFORTS IN TAX PREPARATION RESULT ONLY IN TAX PREPARATION

Proposed Tax Code rewrite. Currently, we are taxing things that we want to encourage, e.g.; business, industry, investment, savings, home ownership, etc. and giving politically determined deductions with often negative consequences. I propose a general structure of a tax code that replaces all federal taxes with a single national sales tax. This would be a tax on all sales to an ultimate consumer. Additionally, the sales tax allows flexibility that an incremental change in the tax rate can accommodate budgetary requirements. Certainly, all the country's best minds must be applied to perfect this code but components are:

- Repeal of the Sixteenth Amendment.

- Use a national sales tax for all government expenses.

- Eliminate all other taxes on Americans including income taxes, business taxes (large and small), and taxes on dividends and interest. (Tariffs are allowed, as appropriate, per Article I, Section 8 of the Constitution, for imported items like oil and drugs.)

- Eliminate all deductions including marriage/child benefits, political contributions, R&D, interest expense, car, home, appliance, energy efficiency,... all deductions. Deductions, rebates and tax breaks become irrelevant if there is no income or business tax.

DON'T TAX WHAT YOU WANT
TO ENCOURAGE

"If I were made king for the day, my first action would be to eliminate the income tax, which is the single biggest barrier to wealth creation faced by Americans today. I would also repeal all laws that regulate commerce between individuals—including, but not limited to the minimum-wage requirement." TAKING BACK AMERICA, by Joseph Farah, p 111.

A flat tax is a potential alternative to a national sales tax and would have many of the same benefits but would continue to tax incomes that we want to encourage. Additionally, if a flat tax is to be fair, it must include all sources of income. Many people (the wealthiest) have their major income from investments and stocks, etc. To tax these elements begins to tax things we want to encourage and introduces political maneuvering into the tax code.

Benefits of the revised tax code:

Benefits foreseen:
- Encourage investment and savings.
- Reduce pre-tax costs of all goods and services.
- Encourage U.S. production capabilities.
- *Reduce exporting of Jobs.*
- Improve balance of trade.
- Remove the financial benefit of marriage so that gay rights people will be more willing to accept that marriage is defined as one man and one woman.
- Reduce the tendency to insure people against their own failures, at the expense of those who act wisely.
- Reduce bookkeeping requirements at all levels.
- Eliminate the IRS
- No longer borrow from future generations, the current Ponzi scheme.
- Reduce Congressional manipulation of the free market.

- Reduce the purpose of Lobbyists and the associated business cost of sponsoring them.
- The rich will no longer be able to avoid taxes by using deductions, loopholes or creating foundations (their charities will be of necessity, charity.)
- The poor may receive welfare to offset the taxes they must pay.

State tax laws are unchanged; they are not the subject of these thoughts.

Reduced Spending Priorities

It has been said and I totally agree that the U.S. Government does not have an income problem; it has a spending problem. A tax increase is not needed but reduced spending is <u>urgently</u> needed. There are ample places to reduce expenditures so that the government can function. Cuts should be made far in excess of anything discussed in Congress.

CUTS BEING CONSIDERED BY
THE 212th CONGRESS ARE
TRIVIAL

Recognizing that cutting all expenditures needed at one time may impact unemployment, I recommend the following sequence of cuts. The first cuts would be to the unconstitutional expenditures, followed by counter-productive activities. A priority of cuts is:

Unconstitutional, eliminate:

- Subsidies to any Media element (First Amendment)

- Earmarks; (Article IV)
- Unemployment benefits (a state function)
- Department of Education (Tenth Amendment)
- Grants to State and Municipal governments; unconstitutional (Article IV)
- All grants and subsidies without constitutional basis
- State Assistance programs (Article IV)

Counter-productive/wasteful, eliminate:

- Alternative energy subsidy
- Oil subsidy
- Farm subsidy
- National Flood Insurance
- Social Security payments to non-needy retirees
- Subsidies for Planned Parenthood, Save the Children, embryonic research, high speed rail, etc.
- All other subsidies and grants without constitutional basis
- IRS (unneeded with revised tax code)
- Numerous duplicative programs and agencies

Severely reduce:

- Unemployment compensation and welfare
- OSHA and EPA
- Homeland Security and FEMA

I believe we should eliminate ALL subsidies. Subsidies, in all cases take money from all, the taxpayer, and give it to the few. Often subsidies take from citizens who have conducted themselves properly and give to those who didn't. I struggle to find any subsidy whose outcome I support; they are mostly for special interests and result from political maneuvering, discussed above.

Discussion

If you budget for it, it will be spent. If you budget for it, you sanction it; if you want more of something, increase its funding and there will be more. Realize that the government bureaucracy is going to "Use it or Lose it." In many cases the government is required to spend money that is budgeted. Therefore, limits on government spending must be initiated by Congress. Funding of many things, e.g. Welfare and Unemployment is a humanitarian necessity, but funding it to a degree that it is desirable is detrimental to the country's survival.

WHY IS THE FEDERAL GOVERNMENT FUNDING PUBLIC BROADCASTING?

"Most Americans have a hard time believing it, but we tax our companies at higher levels that the Europeans tax theirs – You probably didn't know that America is a high-tax country, compared to, say, Sweden. That's because you've been told over and over again that in America we give rich people and businesses a pass. –As in the case of income taxes, corporate taxes don't even bring in as much revenue as they would if they were lower. –Corporations are easy to pick on; that's all.– —one simple reason why politicians avoid reducing corporate taxes; because it looks like a gift to the rich."THE BATTLE by A. C. Brooks, p 85.

I feel that taxpayers would rather tax businesses than people. Business taxes do not come directly out of their pockets. They would rather export jobs and increase unemployment. Legislators appear to agree with them.

THE U.S. GOVERNMENT DOES NOT HAVE AN INCOME PROBLEM, IT HAS A SPENDING PROBLEM

Homeland Security and FEMA. Spending by these agencies is a mockery. The wasteful spending as a result of Hurricane Katrina was sinful. Spending for guards for prevention of terrorism is wasteful when protecting insignificant targets using personnel incapable of thwarting the threat. It is laughable. Spending for construction of 'Fusion Centers' or Residential centers (REX 84) is not only wasteful; it is scary. Building a fence on the Mexican border was wasteful, ineffective and morally degrading.

I know this is controversial, but I believe that legalizing drugs would obviate the need for a fence between the U.S. and Mexico. It would also help Mexico in their fight with the drug gangs. If drugs were legal in the U.S., they would be purchased on the open market and would be more affordable.

With legalized drugs, there would be no motive for the existence of drug gangs. There would be fewer motives for American crime that is committed in order to finance a drug habit. I think it would be a neat trick to legalize drug sale and use in the U.S. but keep the production illegal. This would allow the tax revenue to be gained via a tariff and be consistent with my views on taxation.

I do not believe legal drugs would cause more drug use, if the purchase necessarily required counseling. And, I'm sorry, but I am more concerned for the victims of crimes committed by addicts to support their habit than I am for the addicts.

I think my own experiences in Mississippi and Louisiana make an interesting sidelight. Anyone with any building sense should enjoy the story.

After Hurricane Katrina struck, there was a great movement in sympathy and support for the victims. We felt we should help out if we could.

I did accompany my daughter and son-in-law on a church-sponsored trip to Waveland, Mississippi soon after the storm. We were housed in a large church activity room. We slept on sleeping bags that we brought with us. We helped several people get things back together. We carted furniture and logs to the curb for pickup. We even removed a large tree from the top/side of one home. There was evening camaraderie and fellowship. It was a rewarding experience and I think we helped.

There was one disconcerting feature. One homeowner had requested help. We found a few branches down and my son-in-law took a broken limb out of one tree (I don't think that was storm damage.) He offered us space to eat our sack lunches. During the discussion the homeowner described his interruption from work due to the storm. I believe he said he missed three days of work. But, he happily described the $1000 that he received from FEMA. I believe he said everyone in the area received that amount to cover miscellaneous expenses.

Several months later I went with another church group to Metairie, Louisiana to provide additional help. The church that housed us on this occasion already had air mattresses, presumably left by earlier volunteers. This church provided us with one meal per day. They were very gracious. They had a poster on the wall with signatures of previous volunteers; it was huge, with maybe a thousand names.

This visit was not quite as rewarding. Our team of 10 was asked to work on sheet rocking a home. Only one other man and I had any idea how to work with sheet rock. We reported to the site and learned that we were the third similar group that had worked on sheet rocking this house. We had willing workers but with no experience. One self-starter started vigorously to 'mud' the things she could. She put mud on nails but didn't know that it had to be leveled. The next day, it took at least 10 times as much effort to sand those nail spots as it had taken her to put the mud on them. Oh yes, she mudded joints between sheet rock boards (before they were taped). This effort required a day's delay before the extensive sanding effort could be expended so that the joints could be taped.

My major effort was fixing the seams where wall boards meet the ceiling boards. The previous workgroup had improperly installed the wall boards by first putting a horizontal board on the floor and then setting the next on top of it. This left a gaping hole where the wall boards met the ceiling. Anyone who understands building knows you are supposed to put the first wall board against the ceiling and then lift the lower board to meet it. Those volunteers did not have that experience.

As we worked I realized that plumbing and electrical work was also needed. That should have been done *before* sheet rocking was begun. Also, some windows needed replacing and I could see daylight through one wall. The floor was 4" out of level. My assessment was that the house was not worth repairing; it should have been razed.

When we left there was another crew coming to finish what we did not get done. Let's see, that's three teams of 10. If they each paid $300 for the trip like I, that's 30x$300=$9,000 (labor only) to do a sheet-rocking job, that I, with my contracting experience (Class A building Contractor's License) feel should have cost about $700.

But that's not the whole story. My understanding is that the federal government lent Louisiana an undisclosed amount. I was told that the government forgave that debt based on volunteer work contributed. They forgave at $15 per hour of volunteer work. For 6 days of work at 6 hours per day that is 30x6x6x$15=$16,200 that taxpayers paid for part of the work on *one* house that should have been razed.

But even that's not the whole story. When tax time came my expenses were deductible. I deducted my $300+ as did the remaining 29 people who worked on the one house. At a 25% tax bracket that is 30 people times $300 times 25% = $2,250 that we got back (that other taxpayers paid).

Now the total is $9,000 that the volunteers paid; $16,200 that the federal government (taxpayers) paid and $2,250 that the government (taxpayer) gave back in tax refunds. $9,000+$16,200+$2,250=$27,450 was the cost of a job that could have been done for $700. Worst still is that the house was probably never occupied because it has insufficient structure to be worth repairing, and it is in an area that probably didn't ever recover.

A $700 JOB COST $27,450
WITH GOVERNMENT SUPPORT

Now that was one house sponsored by *one* church that sponsored possibly a thousand volunteers. How much was the federal taxpayer's bill considering the hundreds of churches that sponsored such relief? Was it money properly or efficiently spent?

This trip was not rewarding. Before I had done any of the above calculations, I knew the result. I was in a bad mood during the whole week. I was disillusioned. I want to volunteer and help people in need; but I feel that my volunteer work in this case was actively doing harm.

On another trip to Arkansas to visit my wife's mother, we drove through Hope, Arkansas. We saw a field full of mobile homes. There must have been thousands, all behind a security fence. We turned around for a second look and turned into the driveway to the field. A uniformed security guard looked up and then started to quickly approach our car. We left, but not before we were assured we were not welcome.

For years afterward, I thought that these were excess FEMA trailers not used for Katrina and awaiting another need. I then heard that they may not have been used because there was some formaldehyde in them rendering them unsafe.

Then I read about REX 84. I am not sure to this date what I saw, but the trailers are still there.

No matter what the reason, I see waste.

In another personal experience, I built a solar house in the early 1980's. I was then an active supporter of any manner of reducing our dependence on foreign oil. I may have been categorized as an environmentalist. I worked hard. I designed the system myself.

I bought solar collectors commercially. My biggest pride was that the company selling collectors had their own control "system". After they saw my ideas, they incorporated elements of my design into their own.

With the house complete, I applied for the solar tax credit. I was approved for the maximum credit available, I believe about $20,000.

I lived in the house for several years and monitored its performance. I t worked. It saved some 25% on my utility bills. Given the tax credit it appeared to pay for itself in about 20 years; reasonable success.

Now, looking back on it and realizing how much the government was subsidizing companies developing and producing solar equipment and how much I got back, I am ashamed to have done it.

I contributed to the taking of money from others and took some of it myself.

I am ashamed.

Back to the possible budgetary reductions:

Social Security has become a basic feature in American Society (an entitlement). It does many essential functions in ensuring a given living standard; however, it has definite questionable features. Among those is its support for orphans and widows. Yes, they need support. But the features of the law that deter re-marriage and potential reductions in federal funding must be changed. Too often, a person cannot afford to re-marry due to the loss of income from social security. This is very similar to welfare laws that do not allow a welfare recipient any profit when going back to work.

Social Security should revert to its original intent, a safety net for the poor, <u>not</u> a retirement program. The first cuts to SS would be eliminating payments to people with net worth over ~$1 million.

> Ronald Reagan said, "Before we spend more
> money doing
> what we are doing, we should first determine if
> what we're doing is part of the problem."

Welfare can be reduced by changing rules to require work of able bodied recipients; public works, if other work is unavailable. We must make employment profitable in all cases. I may agree that the government has some roll to play in ensuring a minimal standard of living. However, it is my belief that our current welfare system does not prevent, in fact encourages *systemic* welfare; welfare sometimes continues from generation to generation without an incentive to work. Welfare pays more for more children, but economically discourages marriage.

> "The Great Society has destroyed black families, something even slavery was unable to do. What two World Wars and the great depression were unable to do, the Great Society did in 25 years....the black family in now in shambles", Carey Roberts.

Both Social Security and Welfare are difficult issues but the law *can* be rewritten to prevent the above noted situations.

Medicare expenses can be reduced by eliminating fraud and limiting medical malpractice suits and insurance payments. Medicare and Medicaid should eventually be eliminated in favor of private insurance.

Unemployment compensation should be by private insurance policies as company benefits or through payroll deduction, not by government funds.

Reduce Military budgets for numerous overseas peace-time deployments.

Many Education Department initiatives are counter-productive, causing teachers to teach to the test rather than to educate. All DOE expenses are unconstitutional. Education is a state function.

I would recommend passing the balanced budget amendment, but it would take care of itself with a revised tax code. Any expenditure will result in a change in the sales tax rate, not in deficit spending.

Reduce Federal pay, as needed, to balance the budget. Begin with the President, Congress and the Supreme Court and then include all federal employees including military.

Reduce Social Security and Medicare, if needed.

CHAPTER V

FOREIGN POLICY

We should be helpful, not forceful. We should defend our nation. Recall our troops from foreign nations (yes, including Iraq and Afghanistan) where they are not essential for the defense of America.

I can conceive of a reason for our troops in Germany and Japan. Some troops in these areas can provide a base of future operations, when and if needed. But, Britain, Italy, Spain, Iceland, Chad, etc? Joseph Farah identifies 135 countries where we have troops.

Do not reduce our force structure substantially and be prepared to DEFEND our nation from any *real* threat. Avoid treaties and entanglements. This would help our economy as well as foreign relations.

Do not continue to try to export democracy since it does not work; it is inconsistent with the Moslem faith and we don't have it to export anyway. We have no business in interfering with governments of sovereign nations.

I believe the best things our military have done in recent years, for improved international relations is the support given to Haiti and Japan in surviving their natural disasters.

Planting Democracy, —The U.S. should help the world, not rule the world. It is neither our right nor responsibility to dictate or impose our freedom or government style on others. Culturally, we are all different, and it is only a matter of opinion as to the best form of government in a given location.

Thomas Jefferson said that an informed population is essential to a Democracy. My extrapolation of this is that un-informed voters are subject to manipulation by the Aristocracy. Therefore, an informed population is essential.

King Abdullah of Saudi Arabia said "What we call democracy, the Saudis are liable to call chaos."

Plato said that the best form of government is a Benevolent Dictator.

Nation Building. With the above in mind, we should re-consider our efforts at Nation Building. We should not try to force nations to be re-built, in our image. Most of our costs in Iraq and Afghanistan are from nation building. I believe our military, when required, should limit its actions to stopping the actions of a country that we find to be a threat to our country. Let them rebuild.

We should, however help nations in their own efforts to re-build their nations. We help them in developing a Republican form of government *if that is their desire.* We should make all appropriate non-forceful, non-military efforts possible, if we are to be the Humanitarian Nation that we believe we are.

How powerful could our military be; how securely could they defend our nation if it did not use all its resources in Nation Building.

Historical Perspective. Historical actions and events that are or may be lost from history are discussed below: I include this material because it is of interest to me; that I learned it, not in history books, but from biographies and other study. I include it here not to influence what you believe; I include it because I think you should know it before *you* decide what you believe. And, it might give you some element of humility.

Military as an education, War is hell—and the evidence is below:

In his book, JESSE JAMES, T. J. Stiles describes how the Civil War was an essential element in the development of the Bandit Age. The rigors of war and the horrors of war "violentize" the participants. The James brothers, the Younger brothers and Jim Anderson had to be violentized by the war in order to be ready and able to conduct the "Bushwhacker age" and the following "Bandit age."

As WWII was being won, the horrors of the holocaust were revealed, General Eisenhower ordered all possible photos be taken of German Death Camps and forced German people from the neighboring communities to be ushered through the camps. He wanted to get it on record because "somewhere down the road of history some bastard will get up and say it never happened."

Recently the UK debated removal of the Holocaust from school curriculum because it "offends" the Muslim population which claims it never happened.

"Half the Germans under 24 don't know what the Holocaust was," WHILE EUROPE SLEPT, p 151

In 1904, Without a declaration of war, Japanese torpedo boats surprised Russian ships at Port Arthur and Inchon—a prelude to their victory in the Sino-Russian War. Teddy Roosevelt said "Was not the way the Japs began the fighting Bully? I was thoroughly well pleased with the Japanese victory for Japan is playing our game," IMPERIAL CRUISE, p 214.

His 5th cousin FDR called their similar attack on Pearl Harbor "A Day that will live in Infamy."

I have not found a history book that cites FDR's ultimatum to Japan on November 28, 1941.

"November 28, 1941- It's up to Tokyo now-that's the word from Washington. The fate of the Japanese-American negotiations for settlement in the Pacific depends entirely upon the response that the Mikado's government makes to the terms that the United States has laid down.

From official Sources in the capital we learn that Uncle Sam demands that Japan must consent to get out of China and Indochina and renounce all policies of aggression. The belief is that Tokyo can hardly accept these conditions. So the Japanese-American negotiations would seem to be at the point of collapse." HISTORY AS YOU HEARD IT by Lowell Thomas, p 181.

I am aware of many American mis-deeds. I wonder how many other Americans are. There are many things one cannot find in history books or schools but you can find in written references. Examples:

During the time of WWII, The Nazis were condemned for doing medical experiments on prisoners. In the same time period, the U.S. was conducting medical experiments on prisoners. We were performing lobotomies to calm down mental patients who were hard to control. We were sterilizing people with undesirable traits such as mental retardation and Down 's Syndrome; or for repeated un-wed parenthood. Who is the kettle and who is the pot?

The Moro Crater Massacre; a military engagement of the Philippine-American War, March 10, 1906. U.S. Army forces under the command of Major General Leonard Wood...attacked a village... More than 2000 mostly unarmed Muslim Moro villagers (including many wom-en and children) were killed by the Americans. General Wood called for the extermination of all Filipino Muslims since, according to him; they were "irretrievably fanatical."

Fort Leonard Wood, Missouri was named for this general.

When the Japanese water boarded U.S. personnel in WWII, America tried them for war crimes, IMPERIAL CRUISE, p 107.

President Obama was upset in learning that we were water boarding prisoners in Guantanamo. To his credit, John McCain clearly defined water boarding as torture. I have not heard that the practice has been suspended.

Medal of Honor winner, General Fredrick Funston executed POWs, tortured civilians and raped women and then stoutly defended these tactics (in the Philippines). "I am afraid some people at home will lie awake nights worrying about the ethics of this war, thinking our enemy is fighting for the right of self government....they are semi-savage people, who are waging war, not against tyranny, but against Anglo-Saxon order and decency." "I want no prisoners...the more you kill and burn, the better...kill all over ten years of age." IMPERIAL CRUISE, p 110 & 123.

Japanese horrors of WWII are well documented in FLY-BOYS, by James Bradley

Tests show that soldiers often do not know why they are doing what they do. They certainly do not have an exhaustive knowledge of history, many being 19 years old. Still soldiers have to know the integrity of a mission depends on their obeying orders.

Imperialism. Our country has a strong history of imperialism.

Also attributed to Thomas Jefferson; John O. Sullivan in 1845 spoke of America's "*Manifest Destiny* to overspread the continent allotted by providence for the free development of our multiplying millions."

Most history books document America's progress west overcoming Indian opposition, as well as the war against Mexico memorialized by "Remember the Alamo." The Louisiana Purchase, the Missouri Compromise and states being sequentially recognized as population moved westward. Admiral Perry claimed Hawaii and we bought Alaska. The last state was added in 1959.

One of our last battles with the Indians was at Wounded Knee, S.D. The Indians called it the Massacre of Wounded Knee. Read the book, BURY MY HEART AT WOUNDED KNEE, by Dee Brown, and decide for yourself; as for me, it was a low point of American history.

Teddy Roosevelt supported Japan in taking control of Korea in exchange for Japanese support of American penetration of Asia. IMPERIAL CRUISE, p 170.

We fought a war with Spain. We called it the Spanish American War. The Philippines called it the War of American Aggression.

When we fought in Korea and in Viet Nam, was it totally an effort to stop the dominos of Communist takeover; or was there a residual Imperialistic motive? It is just a question; is there an unorganized effort here like in education, below?

President McKinley was the first president to advance the idea that the U.S. Military invaded foreign countries with benevolent intentions. His logic struck a humanitarian chord and is still embraced today by the American public. IMPERIAL CRUISE, p73&p79.

Are these Imperialistic instincts dead?

Policy statement. *I am unaware of our government's policy on foreign Affairs.* That *scares* me. Am I part of an informed population that is able to vote intelligently if I don't know the foreign policy I am voting for?

George Bush initiated a police action in Iraq, after 10 years there has been no declaration of war. When being advised to have a phased withdrawal from Iraq, he instead made a 30,000 increase in soldiers, a "surge."

Barack Obama campaigned for president calling for withdrawing all troops from Iraq by 2011. He would also close Guantanamo prison in Cuba.

On March 22, 2011 our military was participating in imposing a No-Fly Zone over Libya. In the past weeks we have witnessed a rebellion in Egypt and Civil unrest in Yemen, Bahrain, Syria, Tunisia and Saudi Arabia. The leaders in at least Yemen, Syria and Bahrain brutally put down the unrest. Col. Quaddafi also began to brutally put down unrest in Libya. Why did we choose Libya to be recipient of military intervention?

There has been much discussion of preventing Muammar Quaddafi from killing his own people. As of this date, the mission for the operation is unclear; Are we to depose Quaddafi? Are we to impose a No-Fly Zone or to use military force against Quaddafi's forces? I understand we are to impose the No-Fly Zone, but some U. N. forces have been destroying Quaddafi's offensive capability from the air and there was talk of arming the rebels. What *is* the mission?

If we are successful, what will have been the impact of our actions; what will be the form of a new government; will the new government be what we favor? Do we exchange one despot for another? Are we fighting on the right side?

President Obama did not ask for Congressional approval for his action.

Interestingly, during the Bush administration, now Vice President Biden emphatically said that he would start impeachment actions for President Bush if he did not get Congressional approval of a similar action. Barack Obama reiterated support for that philosophy during his presidential campaign.

I was unaware when I voted for and against each of our last two presidents, what their actions would be. I personally disagree with many of the actions of both. *How was I to know how they would act when I voted?*

What are our motives in Puerto Rico and the Philippines?

I believe most Americans have a view that Americans are good; that what they do in international politics is for the overall good; that we are a Humanitarian Nation. But, recognize that there exists a term, "Ugly American." When reading history, if we read American History from a foreigner's perspective, we must understand their views. We should have some degree of humility when dealing in foreign relations.

I believe we should curtail any residual thoughts of imperialism, if they exist. We need a *Vision Statement of America*. What is important for America? I have not heard of any such statement. Who can establish it? The fact that I can ask these questions and not be certain of the answers shocks me.

We should know what we as a nation stand for. We should agree on our Vision and concentrate our efforts in one direction.

I tried to learn what our foreign policy is. I Googled it and found the National Security Strategy. This 50 page novel was signed by President Obama containing mostly generalities and philosophy. Considering the record of congress passing bills without reading them, I wonder if the President read it. Did Secretary Clinton? Is it being followed? I am sure that most foreign powers do not understand it nor do most Americans.

We need a foreign policy understood by all who are impacted by it.

CHAPTER VI

MEDICAL CARE

America has one of the best, if not the best systems of Medical Care in the world. The technology is there and all Americans have access to emergency medical care. An Emergency Room cannot turn anyone away. This system is much abused but it is there.

I find three faults with American Medical Care. These faults are limited supply, Medical Insurance and Lawyers. The three problems are intermeshed and drive the tremendous cost of medical care and thereby limit its availability.

President Obama made much ado about improving Medical *Care* in America. However, all his efforts were directed to improving Medical *Insurance*. Remember, President Reagan said:

"Before we spend more money doing what we are
doing, we should
first determine if what we're doing is part of
the problem."

Limited supply:

Doctors are in limited supply. I have sometimes had
difficulty in getting an appointment. In one instance
the doctor's office did not open the reservations schedule for the next month until the 15th of the month before.
When I called on the 20th, the next month's appointment
schedule was full so I had to wait another month.

I had a friend with a Master's Degree in engineering who
decided that he really wanted to be a doctor. He couldn't
get into Medical School; there were insufficient spaces
available. I take this as a clear indication that the number of doctors is artificially limited, probably to ensure a
higher level of pay for those selected.

Even without increasing the number of doctors, it would
seem that the supply of medical care could be enhanced
by increasing the authority of nurse practitioners, EMTs
and pharmacies in treatment of minor illnesses.

Medical Insurance:

I believe Medical Insurance *is* the problem in affordable
Medical Care. With insurance the patient has no reason to be concerned about the cost of his care; insurance will pay for it. He is concerned about what his
Co-Pay will be. Competition has been removed from
the medical economy.

Capitalism/competition must be re-introduced into the medical system. A patient should never sign a blank check (with the possible exception of emergency care). When advised of a recommended treatment he should also be advised of the cost. When advised of the cost, *if he were paying directly*, he might simply decline treatment, or he might settle for an alternative treatment or go to a different doctor.

COMPETITION MUST BE RE-INTRODUCED INTO MEDICAL CARE

The customer/patient *must* be directly impacted by this cost to ensure economical care. I believe this *can* be accomplished.

A possible method is that after treatment is recommended, the insurance company, if involved, be advised. The insurance company will then pay the patient something like 50% of the anticipated cost. The patient now has the money and can decide to get the treatment or not. He can ask other medical facilities if they will take his 50%. He can negotiate. That is what is missing in medical care!

A more realistic approach may be to eliminate Medicare Part B and drug benefits. Eliminate similar coverage in insurance policies for the not-yet-retired population. Don't write me off yet!

Do you see the reduction in the Medicare and private insurance premiums? People would pay their own bills for non-hospital care. Most could afford this considering their reduced insurance premiums and this would introduce competition. Doctor's administrative expenses would be lowered.

Realize that in the big picture, what insurance does is level the medical bills. Insurance Companies pay higher medical bills of some customers by using the premiums of those who are not sick, *and they make a profit.* Yes, this seems to leave those who get sick hanging out on a limb. I believe this problem can be addressed by delaying a large bill and spreading it over many years (like using a credit card). Concern must be given for the repeatedly ill person; something like a very high deductible insurance policy? Unusual cases may be supported by Welfare programs.

I have thrown these ideas out for thought; I don't believe these ideas yield the best way to *re-introduce competition*, but are the direction we should move. We need to find the best way.

Lawyers:

Lawyers simply increase the cost of Medical Care. They opportunistically find any way to make money. They sue in the name of a customer but their motive is their own fee or percentage. Opportunities abound; accidents, mistakes, and rare malicious actions. They sue for huge amounts including punitive damages. Their fee is increased.

Doctors must pay huge amounts for Malpractice Insurance. These expenses are of course, passed *directly* to the patient.

I feel many of my points are illustrated by my recent experience. This experience is best illustrated by my own recent experience:

I visited my Cardiologist in December 2011. No problems were found but he recommended I get a stress test.

I had that test in March 2011. While taking the test, I learned that an MRI was now the best way to analyze the results. On previous stress tests the results were evaluated using ultra-sound. My last stress test cost me my $15 co-pay. Since my cost was only $15, I didn't even look at the bill that my insurance company paid.

I received my bill for over $400. Since my bill was much greater than I expected, I further analyzed the bill and found the two hour test cost about $2000. My insurance company payed the difference.

I called to question the bill and was advised that it was my responsibility to know the cost of my treatment.

Some 2 weeks after the test I received a letter say in the stress test "looked good" but my cholesterol medicine should be increased but gave no prescription.

After more than two months, five phone calls and one letter, I have not gotten the recommended

prescription. On my last call the office suggested
I get an appointment to see the doctor again.

I believe my experience illustrates several things. Doctors are not concerned with cost. If a new treatment is
available, they will use it. Doctors prescribe the most ex-
pensive tests and drugs available so they can say they are
giving the best care (and best protection from lawsuits).
They must assume that insurance pays the bill and it is
not of concern to the patient.

Had I had any idea of my own cost, let alone the cost
to my insurance, I would have opted to not have the MRI.
I had no symptoms of a problem and had the test based
only on the doctor's recommendation.

The incremental improvement in my health was not
worth the cost. And, there was a cheaper way to get near-
ly the same level of protection.

If doctors are so busy they cannot answer phone calls
or mail, are they so overworked as to be a danger to their
patients?

Another personal story:

Some years ago we had a next door neighbor who
was in an auto accident. She was hit from behind.
We were next door so we saw her come home from
the hospital, an out-patient visit, wearing a neck
brace. We talked but did not pry into her business.

We observed that she was always at home,
frequently working in the yard and garden. She

did tell us that she always had to be near the phone. After several weeks she quit wearing what we came to call the "Insurance Collar." In a couple of months, she moved away. She had bought a new, much bigger house.

My stories are for illustration, I am sure almost every one can relate similar stories.

I propose limiting the proceedings from all lawsuits to the actual damages, plus the lawyer's fee. Lawyers should be penalized for frivolous lawsuits with fines and disbarment after excessive abuse. Doctors should be liable for these more limited monetary fines but subject to loss of their medical license for excessive abuse.

Of course, we should intensify efforts to eliminate fraudulent claims and increase the penalties.

I propose we repeal the Obamacare *Medical Insurance Reform* and accomplish *Medical Management Reform*. We must make the patient aware of costs and the doctor responsive to the patient without diversions of attention to Insurance and Lawyers.

What do I believe? I believe in capitalism; I believe in Adam Smith's "Natural Price." The natural price is the lowest price at which a product can be produced that gives the provider an adequate return and can be purchased by the patient, under conditions of free competition. I believe our medical system has supply and demand out of balance. I believe the supply side is limited by constrained numbers of doctors and medical facilities and by the high cost of malpractice insurance. Demand is enhanced by medical insurance, the patient being removed from the cost of treatment. I believe these are the areas that Medical Management Reform should address.

I don't have all the answers but I know the direction we should go.

CHAPTER VII

THE WAY WE THINK/EDUCATION

The Way we Think. Why do we think as we do? What makes Liberals; conservatives; right or left? I will describe some of my concerns. My thesis is that the thinking of a population is malleable. It changes with time. It can be changed by circumstances, ideologies or by design; by indoctrination or propaganda. I can't always say what is right, but thoughts dictate our way of life.

When I was young, teachers had some authority. If I was in trouble, the teacher would hit the back of my hand with a ruler. If I persisted, she would spank me. If I got into real trouble at school, that was a minor problem. When I got home, I got in a much bigger problem if my parents found out that I was in trouble at school.

Now, if a child is unhappy with a punishment from parents, often all he/she has to do is complain at school and a Social Services representative will investigate whether the child will be taken from the parents.

When I was a kid, I was instructed to respect my elders. Now, apparently, students are taught to correct them at any opportunity. If I don't wear my seatbelt or if I smoke, young people are quick and often vehement in correcting me.

When I recently chastised a student for posting an unflattering photo of herself on Facebook, she said "I don't care what people think about me." She elaborated that her teachers teach them to not care about what people think about themselves.

When I was young, people were concerned about their "reputations".

Prejudice. We have been prejudiced against blacks. Before that we were prejudiced against Indians. Contemporary with our prejudice against blacks were prejudices against Chinese, Italians, Puerto Ricans, Mexicans, Japanese, WASPS, Gays and others, depending on where you were at the time. Are we over prejudice? Or are we now becoming prejudiced against Moslems? This is included to confirm the malleability of the mind. It keeps changing; what will we think next?

When I was young, in the Jaycees, I learned that ours is a nation of laws. How can we continue if we do not enforce existing laws?

When I was young, my dad sent me out to kill a runt pig. The runt would never be worth anything so I was taught that its life wasn't worth the feed.

Now we have vegetarians. They are sensitive to the feelings of animals. PETA has been quoted as saying that deaths of humans is good because that means less people will be available to eat animals. Where was I wrong?

And there were the Brown Shirts. Hitler instituted this group of youths and indoctrinated them to be Nazis.

The minds of our youth are malleable. What they are told, what they are taught, what they experience determines what they think, what they believe. What they believe determines their future.

Read History or Repeat it. Who rewrites history, why? Text books do not accurately nor exhaustively reflect history. Harry Truman recommended reading biographies to learn history. Michelle Obama said we must rewrite history.

I do believe there is an unorganized effort by people who wish to make America appear to be a humanitarian nation, that they focus a blind eye to unpleasant elements and essentially whitewash history. These people don't want to face reality, and they want to make sure others see history as they do. School boards, state boards of education and the DOE in turn want to be the biggest influence.

In war, it is the winner who writes the history book.

How many Americans read history other than what is taught in school? Yes, they are too busy. They must attend the daily grind and bring home the paycheck to finance their standard of living (generally requiring both parents to work). As I remember my office job, it was quite demanding. It required unpaid overtime and often taking work home.   When I was self employed it was much worse!

When you have time for a little break it is nice to watch TV or read a good mystery; you've earned the break.

November 28, 1941- It's up to Tokyo now-that's the word from Washington.   The fate of the Japanese-American negotiations for settlement in the Pacific depends entirely upon the response that the Mikado's government makes to the terms that the United States has laid down.   From official Sources in the capital we learn that Uncle Sam demands that Japan must consent to get out of China and Indochina and renounce all policies of aggression.   The belief is that Tokyo can hardly accept these conditions.   So the Japanese-American negotiations would seem to be at the point of collapse."   HISTORY AS YOU HEARD IT by Lowell Thomas, p. 181.

How many of you knew that? Can you find a history book that includes it?

How many Americans read any significant number of biographies or relevant history? 5%? 15%?

Education. Public education is considered as essential to this country's existence as the post office.

Benjamin Franklin was appointed as the first Postmaster General by the Second Continental Congress in 1775. Postal service was obviously considered essential to our developing nation.

The earliest education in the country was religious schools in the 1600's. Thomas Jefferson was the first American leader to suggest a public school system. It was primarily the responsibility of the states, and individual school districts. Free public elementary education was available for all American children by the end of the 19th century. In 1983 most states implemented reform strategies to counter low academic achievement in public schools. More frequent state testing was implemented. President Bush introduced his national "No child left behind" plan.

On Fox News, 3/16/2011, Glenn Beck showed a chart of test scores and of federal spending for education. The spending chart showed ever increasing funding over time with test scores almost unchanged.

Ronald Reagan said "Before we spend more money doing what we are doing, we should first determine if what we're doing is part of the problem."

From my own experience, I attended a one-room school for eight years before going to a nearby town for High School. My dad was President of the School Board of the one-room school. I remember his comments when that school was scheduled to be consolidated with others to gain the efficiency of a larger school. He said that would be the death of quality schooling. The year after I graduated, the school was consolidated.

Since that time I have become aware of disturbing practices in school systems; There are panels to decide what books are to be used and the content of these books. This is done at the county, state and National levels.

This reminds me of the book-burnings during the inquisition, also by the KKK.

Michelle Obama said we must rewrite history. History should *not* be rewritten.

READ HISTORY OR REPEAT IT

Federal funding of schools disturbs me greatly. It comes with "strings"; controls. Education was initiated under "primarily state and local" control. I see no constitutional basis other than *"reserved to the States," Amendment X*.

My concerns about quality of education, the rise of home schooling, teachers unions, and other countries having higher test scores at less cost, etc. are beyond the scope of this book.

I do know that the federal money spent is both wasteful and unconstitutional.

Liberal Thinking.

For the life of me, I cannot understand how liberals think.

I am a conservative. I cannot understand how a liberal/progressive thinks. I know that many or most college professors are liberals. This leads terribly to the the shaping of the malleable minds of our youth.

I know that liberals are for a safety net; want to care for the poor; think the rich should pay more. But can they be serious, that they are unconcerned about the National

Debt; that they want to spend anyway? Do they want the country to cease to exist?

Can they be so short sighted to want to continue spending on credit so they can for a few more years live in (relative) luxury? Can they really will their grand-children a devastated world?

I struggled with this and looked for a definition. "Political Night Train," March 2010 defined a liberal; "Generally this is any person who has the following two values, 1) Redistribution of wealth and 2) they truly believe they know what is best for everyone else, regardless of what *they* value or believe."

Liberal activity is a movement toward Socialism. When does American "Change" evolve to the definition of Socialism? Given: SS, Medicare, Medicaid, Obamacare, mergers of Major Airlines and banks and government ownership of GM, Freddie Mac and Fanny Mae. We must have passed the line and *are* a Socialist country.

> "The problem with Socialism is that you eventually run out of other people's *money." Margaret Thatcher.*

Capitalism and free enterprise made this nation, we must retain them.

CHAPTER VIII

WHAT CAN YOU BELIEVE?

News or propaganda/Indoctrination? I've come to believe one cannot believe anything that anyone says; government, media, scientists, anyone. Their individual bias taints anything they say.

"Strongly held opinions often determine what kind of facts people are willing or able to perceive," Melvin Benarde, YOU'VE BEEN HAD, p. 182.

I believe a strong corollary would be, "Strongly held opinions often determine what a person, teacher, newsman or scientist tells someone and what they want you to believe."

Some examples of areas in question follow.

How can President Obama say that Obamacare will save $X billion over the next year when Congress is asked to fund this new law?

I am concerned now about prescription drugs. A recent article hinted that many prescription drugs do not perform as promised. They are only sold to insure profits for the pharmaceutical industry. Who do you believe?

How can the EPA consider CO_2 to be hazardous and control it (at tremendous expense) resulting in the massive Cap and Trade effort while most scientists agree that it is not hazardous?

Asbestos. Asbestos is a classic case of *safety at all costs* and, "Do you believe anything anyone says."

AOL Good News and More, 2/18/2011 had an article titled "Will Canada export Death by Rejuvenating Its Last Asbestos Mine?"

"WILL CANADA EXPORT DEATH?"

In this article AOL cited the World Health Organization estimate of more than 107,000 people dying each year, worldwide from asbestos diseases. They state that inhalation of a single asbestos fiber into the right place in the lungs can be fatal.

A 71-year-old activist said "We don't use asbestos ourselves and are spending millions to remove it from our schools and —yet we are sending it overseas— and telling them it is safe when we know it isn't."

"It is almost beyond belief that a free and democratic nation like Canada is willing to sacrifice human lives in poor and developing nations on the altar of avarice and greed," said Dr. Michael Harbut, chief of the Center for Occupational and Environmental Medicine at Michigan's Karmanos Cancer Institute.

However, politicians, entrepreneurs and bureaucrats in Quebec insist it is perfectly safe, harmless to miners, workers and consumers who handle it.

Canada's Chrysotile Institute insists the material is safe. "It can be used safely in building materials, brake linings and water and sewer pipe."

Residents of the mining district are proud of the miracle material they excavate. None of the town's old-timers ever had anything negative to say about the mines even when heavy white asbestos-filled dust sometimes blanketed the community. They spit on the sidewalk and curse the U.S. Environmental Protection Agency.

The article totally ignores the fact that the U.S. still produces asbestos. Google it, I did.

Class action suits continue to prosecute asbestos producers for ailments of an aging population of people who worked with the product before its dangers were known.

Now, who do you believe? The article acknowledges that it is a political issue.

What do I believe? Since I can't believe anything anyone says, regardless of his education or position, I have to believe what my gut tells me.

SINCE I CAN'T BELIEVE ANYTHING
ANYONE SAYS,
REGARDLESS OF HIS EDUCATION OR POSITION,
I HAVE TO BELIEVE WHAT MY GUT TELLS ME.

I've worked with asbestos periodically in both the fibrous insulation and hardboard and roofing types with no ill effects that would cause me to join the class action suit.

> *I believe* asbestos was harmful in its fibrous form, before any dangers were suspected and precautions taken. I believe it is truly a miracle material. Homes with asbestos siding and roofing survive today after the last manufacture some 50 years ago. Masonite or vinyl siding would not have survived that long; asphalt roofs have been replaced several times in this timeframe (wasting resources and filling landfills). I believe asbestos can be safely produced and used for appropriate uses with responsible precautions, but class action lawsuits continue against companies for actions they made before the asbestos dangers were anticipated.

Ethanol. In the political environment of high gas prices, the term "energy independence" brings in support for anything that proposes *hope* to help reduce our dependence on foreign oil.

The federal government provides substantial subsidies for development and production of wind, solar and other renewable energy sources, principally Ethanol.

There have been studies that indicate that Corn Ethanol uses more BTUs of petroleum energy in its production than the BTUs achieved in its use. This is sufficiently accepted that ethanol producers often stress that theirs is not based on corn but rather rye or other crops.

However, the government continues to subsidize corn ethanol since it is the predominant source of ethanol production. The government mandates that fuel at the pump contain 10% ethanol. I understand that the EPA has raised the 10% rate to 15% to ensure that more ethanol is used.

> Remember, President Reagan said "Before we spend more money doing what we are doing, we should first determine if what we're doing is part of the problem"

There have been objections raised by food and boating industries that ethanol is destructive in many applications. Apparently it is not destructive to internal combustion engines that are used daily, like most automobiles. But for more intermittent uses like Chain saws, lawnmowers, generators and motorboats the corrosive characteristics of ethanol are destructive.

My personal experiences:

> I had to pay over a thousand dollars to rebuild the carburetor on my, almost new, boat.

I paid $89 to replace the carburetor on my lawn mower.

And I paid $187 to repair my house generator.

All this happened in the past year.

I cannot find gasoline that does not contain ethanol.

Ethanol contributes to farm income. It contributes substantially to the cost of food; groceries and meats. The subsidy for ethanol is a hidden additional tax on gasoline at the pump.

WHY ARE WE USING ETHANOL?

Ethanol detracts from the balance of trade. With higher crop prices, reduced exports are an obvious outcome.

Can any unbiased authority state that any of the several renewal energy sources are cost effective? That is, that it produces more energy than is consumed in its total cost of production. Are we seeking the classical (impossible) perpetual energy machine and wasting government funds (taxpayer's money). I have searched for years and cannot find any such authoritative statement. Publicizing such a statement might convince a skeptic like me.

It is obvious that no supportable study has been made that shows a positive cost benefit when considering all factors. If it had been, it would be advertised.

I asked a friend his thoughts about ethanol. His view is that it is a totally wasteful effort that was enacted and continues because of the lobby of farmers.

IS ETHANOL A
PERPETUAL ENERGY MACHINE?

Now, it comes down to what you believe. I have given this great consideration. I have asked authorities. I have listened to my friends and to politicians. In my gut, I believe ethanol will never contribute significantly to the energy equation, *if at all*. It will, however, continue to contribute to increased food costs (inflation) and the federal deficit, *until federal funding is terminated*. I believe wind and solar projects should be pursued wherever they can produce energy **without government subsidy**. I believe that research into alternative energies is critical but subsidizing unproven production is sinful. I believe energy companies should conduct the research without government subsidy.

I believe it is not Politically Correct to shed doubt on the potential of "green energy."

I believe activists are wrong in these cases, as in most cases. I further believe that activists in many or most instances are not really fighting for a cause that they believe in. The activists themselves have not a true feeling for the cause. More likely they like the excitement and are generally revolting against the "establishment." They are being lead by someone or some organization that is striving for minority rule.

Safety and Environmentalism. The country is overly concerned about safety and environmentalism. When these issues are mentioned, no cost is considered.

It is not that safety is not important but it is that it is overdone.

Safety has negative impacts; I believe the extent of safety awareness is counter-productive. I believe people are responsible for their own safety, within limits. When safety is supreme, people lose the responsibility for their own safety. If there is a problem, they sue.

There is not much to say about automobile safety, except that the numerous recalls and safety requirements add to the cost of the automobile. When roads are under construction, I do believe there are more workers devoted to the safety aspects than the construction. Traffic control cones may extend for miles.

In constructing tall buildings, safety fences and halters are required. No expense is spared. Whatever happened to the Mohawk Indians noted for skill in constructing New York's skyscrapers?

We must recall some items that *may* collapse *if* improperly assembled. There are numerous other cases of safety *overkill*.

OSHA and the EPA proliferate safety rules. Their budgets should be cut or the agencies *terminated*.

Safety information is required. I am sure that most printed and publicized safety information is given *only as a precaution against lawsuits*. The information is so predominant that it is not read. It is so lengthy it can hardly be understood. It is often wasteful of the time required for its preparation and of the paper it is written on. Some over-done safety information is:

A *permanent* sign on a sidewalk in a nearby shopping center says the sidewalk may be slick under conditions of ice, rain or snow. It is wasteful of material and is an eyesore.

Use Caution

**All Walkways, including sidewalks and
Parking areas may be slippery and may
Result in an injurious fall**

There is a Risk, You must use caution

Use Caution

You can bet that at some time, somebody sued over the issue, and that resulted in the signs.

The government *requires* restaurants to post; "Consuming raw or undercooked meats, poultry, seafood, shell food, or eggs may increase your risk of food borne illness..."

Airlines are required to give the safety brief. Even though there is no smoking on the entire airplane they must say that "smoking is prohibited in the restrooms and that tampering with the smoke detector....." Do they even have smoke detectors in the restrooms anymore? The required statement is at least 25 years old. If they have to say anything, please make it relevant.

I bought a can of Round-up to kill weeds. I've used it hundreds of times. All I needed to know was how much of this concentration was required to mix with a gallon of water. It wasn't printed on the outside so I had to open the stick-down pages. That information was hidden on page 3, between safety instructions on pages 1 and 2 and disposal cautions on page 4. I had to go to the house and get a pair of glasses so I could read the small print. Need I say more?

At least 50% of any instruction or assembly manual is devoted to safety; it is a waste of paper. Worse, it makes it very difficult to find the information that is needed.

Is there no limit on the amount of money available? If money is limited, money spent wastefully could be used for another need. *Perhaps money saved could go toward Social Security or reducing the national debt.*

IF SAFETY IS MENTIONED, COST IS IMMATERIAL

On March 24, 2011, an air traffic controller at Washington (Reagan) National Airport dozed off on the job. Recordings of the pilots of two planes' (in the air at the time) radio conversations were televised. The pilots discussed why the tower didn't respond then proceeded to land. It was the middle of the night and no other planes were around. News commentators discussed the dangers..... An FAA spokesman said such failure was inexcusable; the FAA would ensure that no tower would in the future be manned with only one controller. An experienced pilot was interviewed. He said the incident resulted in no increased danger; that pilots often land at airports that have no control tower operations. Another expert, an author, said it didn't matter how much it cost, such things cannot happen.

The FAA action was a knee-jerk reaction.

On April 14, 2011, Fox news reported that another air traffic controller fell asleep on the job; this time in Reno, Nevada. Again the sole plane in the area landed safely after failing to reach the tower. Again, the issue was to have two controllers at all times; just *add the cost to the National Debt.*

To alleviate the problem I would suggest that control towers be closed at times when the air traffic is known to be small. This would *SAVE* taxpayer money.

I am curious about two things:

> What is the rule that says that when new cars have automatic door locks they engage when the auto reaches 15 MPH? I believe door latches are sufficiently sturdy to prevent opening in case of an accident, without being locked. Being locked appears to me to mean you may not be able to get out of the car if you have an accident in water. If your accident is on land, you are required to unlock the door in order to get out; an unnecessary extra step. What happens if there is an electrical problem and the door will not unlock; what happens if someone outside tries to save you? I am curious who made this requirement and why.

> Next, seat belts: I recently had an overweight and almost disabled friend in my car. He was in the back seat of my full sized sedan. He dutifully wore his seat belt, in accordance with the law. When we arrived at our destination, I helped him out of

the car; he could not get to the seat belt latch. I struggled to reach the latch; it took a full minute to get him out of the car. In case of an accident—?

America, the land of the free. The government tells how fast to drive; what you can hear or say; what you can wear, smoke, drink; what light bulb you can use; what is taught in schools; what is broadcast on your news, etc. When does freedom end and the government take over? When the government acts, freedom is reduced.

I read a document based on Forbes Money Magazine. "15 Ridiculous Warning Labels." Hilarious! Warnings presumed to help in avoiding lawsuits.

> "There's no trick to being a humorist
> when you have the whole government
> working for you."
> Will Rogers

I have to agree, sometimes watching Fox News, I have to wonder if what I'm hearing should be on the Comedy Channel; in fact it often is.

CHAPTER IX
DANGERS

The country is currently suffering under the Great Recession (the bell ringer).

Remember the Great Depression? Of course not, you weren't yet born. Circumstances were different then. During the Great Depression, there was no 'safety net'. There was neither Social Security nor Medicare, 24.8% of the people were unemployed. There were breadlines.

My father said "It is a depression if it is YOU who lost your job". There were then as now many who did not lose their jobs. They benefited greatly from the depression. They bought farms for pennies on the dollar. It appears to me that those who currently are employed are benefiting greatly from our "recession." Record salaries, cheap homes–.

During the Depression there were breadlines but 60% of Americans lived on farms and many could eat off the land. They didn't like the depression but they survived. My Mother learned to hate eating chicken. Chicken was almost the only meat she had to eat during the depression.

Now 75% of the population lives in an urban environment. If things got really tight, where would they get food? We are an interdependent society. Really we are a dependent society. We depend on technology and economy.

Other concerns:

Minority Rule.

Current events include riots and demonstrations in numerous Arab/Muslin countries. There is no doubt that the demonstrators want to change the way their governments work.

There is no indication that the demonstrators are in the majority in their countries. The Muslim Brotherhood. In Egypt is said to have 30% support of the general population.

They are a minority but they want to change things; to decide who should rule; or to rule themselves. The fear is that, as an active minority, they will achieve leadership; Rule?

Now, in Wisconsin, the recent election gave Republicans the majority in the Senate. The Democratic minority decided to be absent so that a quorum could not be made in order to pass a budget design they did not support. Democrats are a minority but they want their minority vote to be decisive. Do they want to institutionalize minority rule?

Similar activities seem to be happening in Indiana and Michigan.

I fear that the U.S. Senate filibuster is another attempt for minority rule.

There has been discussion for years about the Silent Majority. I think this discussion often was meant "listen to them now, but at the election, the majority will rule". I'm not so sure. The squeaky wheel gets the oil. Minorities ARE ruling in many (most?) cases.

History shows that the Nazi movement had support of 30% of the German people. Stalin had 5% support. I have not been able to find an accurate figure of the support that Mao Zedong had; I can only find that "With a small force, Mao was able to ....."

I understand civil rights and protection of minority rights but I don't accept minority rule.

<u>Fragile Technology</u>.

Technological growth, in the past 100 years, has been phenomenal. Also in the past 50 years; the last 25 years; 5 years.

We are an interdependent society but we have become a dependent society. We have come to depend upon technology. Banks have few bookkeepers. Businesses have laid off their clerks and telephone operators. Computers have made these jobs unnecessary. Food distribution depends on trucks, trains, planes and ships.

We should be concerned with High Altitude Electromagnetic Pulse (HAEMP). There was a report on FOX News on 2/18/2010 that an estimate of the damage from an HAEMP event could kill 90% of the U.S. population due to the disruption of communications, transportation, etc.

If the conduit moving water from the Colorado river were broken, people in Los Angeles would die of thirst. They would not have time to evacuate the city. They would have nowhere to go. If the Colorado river dried up?

Any kind of significant war or even economic turmoil or war could have substantial disruptions in the interdependent society that is dependent on continuity of energy, transportation, communications, data, etc. could have disastrous results.

If the trucking industry failed, New Yorkers would starve.

In a real economic crisis, maybe a depression, could the trucking industries go bankrupt or not be able to afford fuel?

I have a fear that science will be the end of us all.

Doctors. With all the best of intents, I believe that doctors, in net and in the long run, increase the net pain of the elderly. Already, the extension and preservation of life causes more lingering death to many. In the long run, there will be more people to suffer.

I believe excessive caution may be counter-productive. Specifically, the great emphasis on cleanliness.

When I was a kid, I cleaned out hog houses; it washed off! My body developed its immune system. I believe people today who are diligently clean may be destroying their immune system. Evidence of this is the evolution of anti-biotic resistant bacteria in hospitals. I fear that when an epidemic does arise, people will have reduced natural immunity, and they may not survive.

Recent news said Measles is on the rise. Polio has not been eradicated.

Scientists. Scientists are not perfect so that there is a chance that they will make a mistake. Some of the things they are working on can have disastrous impacts it they make a mistake. They make something toxic to (honeybees?), all honey bees die. It upsets the balance of nature; corn and wheat no longer produce; huge populations starve. Work on genetics, etc., not to mention nuclear dangers.

Knowledge. I thought long and hard whether to include this section here or in the chapters on "The Way We Think/Education" or "'What you can Believe." I think it is properly in the Danger chapter.

I have tried to say that you often cannot believe what you hear or read. I have come to the conclusion that the bias embedded in the news, papers, and books is quite intentional. Newsmen, authors and educators *want* to influence what you think. In this they want to influence how you act; and thus the direction of the country.

WHAT DO YOU BELIEVE?
WHY?

I admit it. The reason I am writing is to try to influence how you think, what you believe. Other writers and speakers will also admit it. My point in bringing it up is that you should be *aware* that you are intentionally being led. What I ask is that you notice the source of the information that you are absorbing and think about how it is making you think.

When you listen to a news anchor, I believe you should ask yourself what is it he is trying to make me believe? Why isn't he covering a current event of your interest? I believe you should try to hear other perspectives before you establish your own beliefs. You should listen to and read various news sources.

Current news is confusing. At one time I hear it is $90 million and another $430million that the federal government is providing in support of the Public Broadcasting System. The reason I address this in the DANGER chapter is that it *scares* me to think our government wants to support *and influence* any Media work.

DOES OUR GOVERNMENT
INFLUENCE THE MEDIA?

Before you trust what you yourself think, you must see and consider other points of view. Don't be too busy to notice.

A personal note. On August 8, 1974, I was employed in a hectic office; I was busy, often working unpaid overtime. We were raising two small girls. I was home from the office and we were playing with the kids; taking pictures. It was sometime later when looking at the photos, we noticed we had a picture of our television. On the screen, it was showing Richard Nixon giving his resignation speech. I had been too busy to notice when it happened. I was not informed on current events and probably should not have been qualified to vote.

How do you know what to believe? Worse yet, how do you trust what you think? When you look at the information provided to you through schools and media and people; when you realize that governments sometimes fund the media and at other times instruct schools in what not to put in text books; when you hear "reputable people" say things you know are untrue; when you realize the school books you read excluded information; how do you trust what *you* think?

Don't develop too strongly a position on an issue or cause just because of something you are told or read. Be careful in deciding what to believe.

"Wisdom is supreme; therefore get wisdom. Though it costs all you have, get understanding." Proverbs 4:7.

Have you noticed when you are in public, perhaps another person is working the cross-word puzzle you just finished? He is reading the newspaper that you are going to read, or a book you have read. Realize that the people who want to change the way you think are reaching everybody. In a way, that is good but in a way that is dangerous.

Absurdity of Political Correctness. Yes, I do consider political correctness a danger to our nation. A friend told me that political correctness often prevents the truth from being stated; I pursued that idea. If the truth cannot be said, how can a proper decision be made?

IF THE TRUTH MIGHT OFFEND SOMEONE IT CANNOT BE SPOKEN

To first address a sensitive political correctness issue, let's talk about African Americans. Yes, this is sensitive because I might say something that is not Politically Correct.

It is politically correct to refer to American citizens of a black race who are often descendents of American slaves as African Americans. It seems that this is the preferred designation.

In earlier times these people were referred to progressively as Niggers, Darkies, Negros, Coloreds and Blacks. They didn't really have much to say about being called Niggers or Darkies; it was more acceptable to be called Negros. At a point in time between Reconstruction and the civil rights improvements in the 1960's, it be known that they would rather be referred to as Blacks; the earlier designations were now offensive. Those names were definitely not politically correct. I didn't really notice when it was decided that African American was the preferred term. "Black" is now offensive.

Now if we want to talk about the truth, Black might refer to Caribbean, Indonesian, Pakistani, Philippine or other designation. So Black is both politically and factually incorrect.

Nigger or Darkie are of course derisive terms that never had a positive value.

But African American? That might refer to an Arab. I met a white woman born and raised in South Africa, a citizen of South Africa. She is now an American citizen. She is an African American.

Many of the black American citizens' heritages are from the Niger River Valley so that the term Negro may have been proper in some cases. Those whose heritage is Ethiopia may properly be Ethiopian American; others might be Congolese American; Sudanese American; etc.

I personally think Black is the most descriptive and inoffensive term to describe African Americans, *if any term is needed*. But I recognize that term is no longer politically correct. Why not just American?

I know this is a sensitive issue and I really have no stand on it. Except that it is a graphic illustration that political correctness can disguise the truth.

In my own case, what am I? Am I Irish American; am I African American, WASP, Native American, or Scotch Irish. Maybe, maybe in part, probably all. But I really don't know. I do know that I am an American because I was born here and I live here, period. It is interesting to study genealogy, but what ultimately matters is not my ancestry but who I am.

THE ABSURDITY OF POLITICAL CORRECTNESS

Another personal note: I was a smoker. I lived the life of changing smoking rules. I've heard of the decisions being made in "smoke filled rooms". I participated in some.

When I went to college, it was up to the professor if smoking was permitted in class. Do you believe it? It is true. I worked in a workplace for years where smoker's rights prevailed. The rules changed; we were segregated, smokers in one area and non-smokers in another. Next, we could only smoke in private offices, then only in stairways or outside.

Interestingly when smokers were isolated to stairwells, or outside, unique associations were made. If a worker and a manager both smoked, they had free communication. A unique feature. And it still happens.

> Newsweek, March 21, 2011, page 49, "Oklahoma's Tom Cole enjoys hanging with the 'cigar caucus,' House members who retreat... for smoke breaks. 'You sit down together with a cigar,' insists Cole, 'and you'll have a relationship with somebody at the end of it.'"

I knew of a cigarette company study that concluded that smokers were more productive than non-smokers. I heard the presidents of several cigarette companies testify in front of Congress. To a man, they affirmed that smoking was not addictive.

Subsequently, Class-Action-Suits abounded. People who knew smoking was dangerous were able to sue and get reimbursed for medical expenses or beneficiary benefits if someone died.

Now what do I believe? Well, I believe smoking is bad for your health. I believe that the company presidents lied. But, I believe the study was true; that smokers were more productive. I believe the lawsuits against the cigarette industry were immoral. But, they were Politically Correct, at that time. Tobacco made this country. Why not sue McDonalds, et al. I believe health problems are greater in that arena than in the tobacco industry. Again, since I can't believe what I hear, I have to go with my gut feeling.

Political correctness rules; truth is irrelevant.

Where did political correctness come from? Was it a response to random name calling? Is it primarily an inter-racial thing? Or does it stem from cultural conflicts. I really don't know its source. I'll Google it!

Wikipedia says political correctness is..." language, ideas, policies and behavior seen as seeking to minimize social and institutional offense in language, ideas, policies, and behavior seen as seeking to minimize social and institutional offense in occupational, gender, racial, cultural.....contexts and doing so to an excessive extent.

Examples:
"Mentally Challenged" in place of "Retarded"
"African American" in place of "Black" or "Negro"
Gender-neutral terms such as "firefighter" in place of "fireman"

Terms of disability; "visually challenged" or "hearing impaired" instead of "blind" or "deaf."

Wikipedia did not illustrate "vertically challenged" in lieu of "short" or "weight challenged" in lieu of "obese."

It did however state that terms like "niggers, coons, dagos, wogs, poofs, spastics, and sheilas" have become heresy.

And, that Political Correctness is merely the resentment of spoilt children directed against their parent's values.

Wow! It is truly amazing what you learn when researching to write a book. I have come to believe Political Correctness is a problem. Wikipedia already knew it. They call it absurd!

Why do we use PC if it is known to be absurd? The silent majority doesn't want to offend? Or, are we simply afraid of the reaction of someone offended. Do we really want minority rule in this country?

PC says we can't call Islam a terrorist religion-we must defeat political correctness before we can defeat the Islam threat.

In response to the "Islamic terrorism" that resulted in 9/11, President Bush declared a war on "Terrorism."

A friend said "If we in the West recognize the Islamic threat, we can defeat it. Political correctness says we can't call Islam a terrorist religion-so we have to defeat political correctness first. Political correctness does not allow the truth to be said."

TO EFFECTIVELY DEAL WITH
ISSUES OF NATIONAL SURVIVAL
WE MUST DEFEAT POLITICAL CORRECTNESS
FIRST

We lived in Michigan in 1970. There was a presidential election. Now, we had just moved from Arkansas and Missouri. George Wallace was a third party candidate for president. I favored Wallace. I would mention favoring Wallace at a party and people would look around to see if anyone heard. They appeared shocked that I might even consider being for Wallace. That was not politically correct.

Well, Wallace took the state of Michigan in the election.

On March 16, 2011, I listened to Glenn Beck. He said the "Three Little Pigs" has been rewritten to be more politically correct. The story is now ecologically and morally PC. One of the houses was built from "recycled materials" rather than of "straw." And the three pigs successfully convinced the wolf that his evil ways were wrong; that he should be a nice wolf.

The moral had been totally changed from "self accomplishment" to "ecology and charity" – *from free enterprise to socialism.*

I believe Political Correctness has intersected with, "Read History or Repeat it."

What about Little Black Sambo and Enie Menie Miney Mo? I bet you don't even know what I mean.

By the way, Webster's definition of political correctness is "conforming or adhering to what is regarded as ortho-dox *liberal* opinion on matters of sexuality, race, etc....", TAKING BACK AMERICA by Joseph Farah,   p 187.

CHAPTER X

CONSTITUTIONAL AMENDMENTS

Recognizing that these constitutional amendments are impossible because they are not in the self interest of those empowered to make these amendments, I will propose them anyway.

Term Limits. Revise the 22nd amendment to read: "No person shall be elected to any specific federal office more than twice."

Numbers in Congress. Revise the constitution to allow one Senator per state and 100 Representatives based on population, each state will have at least one Representative.

Poll Test. Revise the constitution to require a test of all voters. The test should ensure that the voter understands the Constitution, the organization of government and current events.

Free Enterprise. Amend the constitution to sustain the vision of free enterprise.

Discussion

Term limits would foster a representative government instead of professional politicians.

Numbers in congress would eliminate most congressional districts, gerrymandering and much political maneuvering. I believe that fewer Congressmen would *improve* representation of the people; it would make decision making easier and reduce Political Maneuvering. As a bonus, it would reduce costs.

A poll test may prevent the coming suicide of our democracy. Of course there is difficulty in deciding who should write the test; it can be overcome. See ANNEX I.

A poll test is not prohibited by the Constitution. The Constitution does not mention voting; by exclusion it left this right to the discretion of the States. As part of the civil rights movement in the 1960's the voting rights act of 1965 made a poll test illegal. The law would have to be changed, as a minimum. The voting rights act, in itself may well be unconstitutional.

What is the vision of the country? Is it free enterprise or socialism? Do we want free enterprise or is our country being ruled by a minority that wants socialism? The Free Enterprise amendment may not pass but we should consider the question and set our course so that we are going in one direction and don't go back and forth based on the latest election or political maneuver.

An amendment to insure that a law applies to all citizens is not needed, we just need to enforce existing laws and follow the constitution.

I believe congress should pass numerous constitutional amendments. Constitutional amendments would replace many laws. The advantage is that an amendment would set the course of the country. A law can be changed by the next administration with a simple majority or an Executive decision. An election won by a 1% margin should not be sufficient to give excessive powers to the winners.

Overriding the constitution requires two-thirds vote of both House and Senate and approval of the States; and, thus, would maintain some stability in government.

The first amendment of this nature should define our foreign (military) policy. See APPENDIX III.

I struggle thinking of other possible amendments to constrain the assumption of powers by the president; to limit the Supreme Court to Federal level Constitutional issues and the written law; and to force Congress to assume its proper role in writing laws. I would like to limit the physical word count of laws so they can be understood. First we need to move in the right direction before we can complete the Vision of America.

CHAPTER XI
PARTY PLATFORM

These thoughts are summarized in an action plan. I call it a Party Platform-What We Should Do.

Party Platform:

Change the focus. Follow the Constitution or change it. Follow the intents of the founding fathers. Leave state functions to the states. Be friendly, not forceful in foreign Relations. Eliminate government debt. Enforce or change all laws.

Planks:

- Repeal the Sixteenth Amendment to the Constitution.
- Rewrite Tax Code.
- Eliminate the IRS.
- Reduce unemployment and welfare benefits.[1]
- Make all actions applicable to all states.[2]

- Eliminate all rebates, subsidies and tax credits.
- Do not reward bad behavior.[3]
- Legalize, tax (tariff) and control all drugs.[4]
- Enforce existing laws, or change them.[5]
- Revise the judicial system to ensure prompt and speedy trial. Eliminate excessive penalties.
- Do not address moral issues.[6]
- Regulation to minimize medical tort and fraud.
- Medicare and Medicaid should revert to competitive insurance policies.
- Repeal Obamacare and pursue Health Care Management reform.
- Begin a program of review of existing laws for a constitutional basis.
- Cease funding the Media; prohibit federal influence.
- Social Security phased back to its original intent.[7]
- Invoke the Sherman anti-trust Law and prevent conglomerates that can become "too big to fail."
- Eliminate the Department of Education, both wasteful and a state function.
- Study the elimination or serious reduction of Homeland security and FEMA; FCC, USAF, DOT, FAA.[8]
- Initiate Constitutional Amendments for: Term Limits, Numbers in Congress, A Poll Test, and Free Enterprise. Consider other Amendments.
- Write a National Foreign Policy, in less than five pages.
- Write a National Military Policy, in less than five pages.
- Renounce Imperialism and cease efforts in Nation Building and Exporting Democracy.
- Revise the Constitution to reflect the National Vision.

Notes:

[1] Reduced Unemployment benefits not only reduces expenditures but it gives an Incentive to go back to work even at a reduced wage. Welfare, likewise, must be reduced to not give incentives for continuing inactivity. Public service should be required of all able bodied, unemployed and welfare recipients to offset state and local government expenses for varied services (trash removal, roadway maintenance, etc).

[2] Nothing should be done for the benefit of a specific state or group. Earmarks will be illegal, freeing congressmen's time for the country's business.

[3] Capitalism includes the right to fail. Do not subsidize people who should fail at the expense of those who acted properly.

[4] Accept the fact that there are and will be users. Undercut the dealers and smugglers and make the world safer. And get increased federal revenue.

[5] Specifically, immigration, slander and libel. Ensure that all laws are applicable to all citizens, including politicians.

[6] Moral issues are religious issues. Government should not take a stand on abortion, gay rights, etc. It is not up to government to tell others what to do; to restrict their freedoms. Certainly the government should not fund issues if morals are in question.

[7] A minimal sustenance for those who have nothing else; not a retirement program. People with adequate

other income will not receive SS. Retirement aspects could be replaced with a time-phased conversion to a private contributory retirement program.

[8] Many of these agencies should be state functions. Others have duplicative or unnecessary functions.

CHAPTER XII
CAN AMERICA SUSTAIN PROSPERITY?

No.

My theory, chapter 1, says no. In the long run, I do not believe it is possible to sustain prosperity.

In the short run, it is possible to extend the selfishness (or gambling) phase (see page 27) but I believe we need *immediate action* to prevent a prompt end to American prosperity.

Our government is out of control.

The answer to every problem is more spending without ever looking back to see if old spending decisions are still correct; is the EEOC still needed?

Laws are too long. They are too long to be understood by legislators who enact them and too long for the people impacted to understand.

The government gets into our personal lives too much; the DOJ sues *individual* people. The government is so big it does not understand itself. There is no vision.

If this book does not describe the changes needed, our leaders must put their higher intellect together and figure out what changes are needed; but they cannot continue to do business as usual.

In initial drafts of this book I kept using the phrase, "It is hopeless." My wife said that was too pessimistic, so I changed the words to "Reasons for Concern".

Without **major** change, I do believe it is hopeless. There is optimism that there can be major change. I may not live to see the inevitable but my grand-children will.

America, the land of the free. The government tells how fast to drive; what you can hear or say; what you can wear, smoke, drink; what light bulb you can use; what is taught in schools; what is broadcast on your news, etc. When government acts, freedoms disappear.

LEGISLATORS' ACTIONS ARE NOT IN THE SELF-INTEREST OF THEIR GRAND-CHILDREN

Government's principle function is the defense of our nation. What are the threats that we face. I believe the most serious threat to America is to its economy. With recent news of Wiki-leaks, hacking into Iran's nuclear capability, and HAEMP; the cyber threat is ominous. America has undisputedly the greatest armed forces in the world. We should recognize that nothing we have, not Social Security, not Medical care is worth the loss of our country. We must do whatever is needed to prevent that.

THREATS TO OUR NATION ARE:

1. Economy
2. Knowledge/Political Correctness
3. Military

We must have good information and proper understanding in order to know what it is we should do. We must know what to believe. Our education system needs good teachers and needs to teach relevant information; true history. We must be aware of the threats of Socialism, Multiculturalism and political correctness.

"Unless we overcome the forces of political correctness and honestly discuss the dangers of radical Islamism, we will never develop what Roosevelt and Churchill would have called a Grand National Strategy to defeat it. And without that, we are unlikely to win." Newt.org/issues, April 6, 2011.

It disturbs me tremendously that I don't know what our National Military Objectives are, but that I can vote.

It disturbs me that our voting population is not well-informed and often not even aware. I believe efforts by political parties, unions, PACs to get out the vote or in any other manner to influence how others vote, are immoral. It is taking advantage of the lack of knowledge of voters.

Is our government doing its principle function well; is it defending our nation? Are we properly prioritizing our efforts?

OSAMA BIN LADEN SAID
HE WOULD BANKRUPT US

I am not in a position to know if we are doing well in our cyber war. I believe we are doing well militarily, but I know we are losing the biggest war, the economic war.

The *system* is broken. Will Rogers and Ayn Rand tell us clearly that this is not a new problem. Our government is taking our Nation aggressively in the wrong direction. Change is needed now if there is any chance of the Survival of America.

Is our biggest danger our leadership and Political Quagmire?

Will the changes be easy?

No.

Change will be difficult. Government is too ingrained in greed; too big to change, particularly when those who want change are the Silent Majority. We are so silent we don't want to be identified as wanting change—we may offend some radical! I bought signs saying "No Incumbents" and found no one who would display the sign... Even those who want change don't want it enough to get up off the couch, to not be Politically Correct! But those who want Minority rule are active. Remember, the squeaky wheel gets the grease.

Also, I read Obama's book, THE AUDACITY OF HOPE, written before the election. People voted him in anyway.

The Silent Majority does not yet understand that *Minorities do rule* this country.

MINORITIES RULE
THIS COUNTRY

I believe the change to the tax code is essential, but the reduced expenditures will not come without pain.

Reducing the size of government and eliminating unnecessary or inappropriate functions will put people out of work. The tax code rewrite will reduce exporting of jobs and increase business employment. Time phasing of the change will determine if unemployment will go up or down. The net change should be a change of employment from the government sector to the private sector and hopefully a large increase.

The people who strive for minority rule will object: There will be resistance from all special interests. Unions will resist; the Bar Association will find innumerable legal objections. Accountants will surely establish a PAC to resist the income tax law revision; many of them would lose their jobs.

Colleges will go ballistic.

If we defeat Political Correctness in order to see truth, we may upset some uninformed people.

The vision of our country is its Constitution. Complete the Vision by amending it.

I do not advocate a constitutional convention. With the current diverse points of view, it would not be possible; we cannot write a Vision for America. We must stay with the founders' vision; that is what made America great. We must write our country's Vision as incremental changes to the Constitution.

We should return to limited government and free market economy.

ANNEX I

POLL TEST

I believe a poll test *can* be developed in a manner that can be accepted by the majority of Americans. A poll test that will ensure that Americans have some basic education, understanding of America, and knowledge of candidates' values.

I propose that each candidate publish a "fact sheet". The candidate is free to put anything on that one-page document that he wants; he can convey it to voters as he wishes but all polling places will have the fact sheets available for anyone who did not get it otherwise.

The fact sheet must contain four statements containing the phrases, "I am for" or "I am against."

For the test a computer will randomly reverse 50% of the "I am for" or "I am against" statements of each candidate.

The voter will go to the voting booth and take a test, *in English*, consisting of one T/F question relating to each candidate and one multiple choice question such as the one below. Missing more than one of the questions will invalidate his vote.

The Multiple choice question would be something like: The American Government is made up of a Legislative branch, a Judicial Branch and an:

> A. Economics Branch
> B. Education Branch
> C. Executive Branch
> D. Defense Branch

The computer will randomly change the position of the correct answer; it may be reasonable for the computer to randomly change the multiple choice question among several similar questions.

The test is not perfect but it would insure some level of consideration and understanding of the voter. Fear of the test may even cause the voter to study for the test; for the election.

An alternative approach might be that proof of passing the U. S. Citizenship test be required to be eligible to vote.

ANNEX II
SELF TEST

I felt it would be of interest to query your own views. The test has no scientific basis, but is intended for further self-evaluation.

TEST

How many proposed constitutional amendments, page 80, would you support? (Circle One answer)

0

1

2

3

4

More than 4

For assessment of your answer, see next page.

ASSESSMENT

If you circled:

    0   You have not read the book.
    1   I've made you think
    2   You can think for yourself
    3   You are a conservative
    4   You favor survival of America
   5+ You favor constitutional definition of a new vision of America

ANNEX III
FOREIGN (MILITARY) POLICY

This is a statement of the foreign military policy of the United States of America. It is made to solidify our own goals so that our citizens know what to expect from their government. It informs foreign powers as well.

It will be short enough to be understood and implemented.

This statement can be made as a law, a political platform or a constitutional amendment; I prefer the latter.

Contents of course must be agreed to, but I propose:

- The United States Military has the primary function of defending our nation.

- America renounces any Imperialistic motives.

- Armed forces will not be used without an order by the President with confirmation by the Senate, except to repel an attack.

- Conflict will not exceed 60 days without a declaration of *war*.

- Sovereignty of nations will be respected.

- In defense of our nation, after appropriate diplomatic efforts, force will be used when necessary to eliminate threats to our Nation, subject to Presidential order with Senate confirmation.

- If force is used, it will only be used to eliminate the threat. Rebuilding or reorganizing a foreign nation is not a military function.

- Stationing of U. S. Forces in any sovereign nation will only occur by specific invitation by that nation.

- American military power is available for humanitarian services if not otherwise engaged.

ANNEX IV

The Constitution is added as an annex to this book, because it is so often referenced. I have added italics at certain places to make cross referencing to the book easier. Its inclusion may also add to the value of the book, since you might have paid almost as much for a copy of the Constitution as you paid for this book. Also, I think everyone needs to have a copy.

THE CONSTITUTION OF THE UNITED STATES

WE THE PEOPLE of the United States, in Order to form a more perfect Union, establish Justice, insure domestic Tranquility, provide for the common defense, promote the general Welfare, and secure the Blessings of Liberty to ourselves and our Posterity, do ordain and establish this Constitution for the United States of America.

Article. I.

Section. 1. All legislative Powers herein granted shall be vested in a *Congress* of the United States, which shall consist of a Senate and House of Representatives.

Section. 2. The ***House of Representatives*** shall be composed of Members chosen *every second* Year by the People of the several States, and the Electors in each State shall have the Qualifications requisite for Electors of the most numerous Branch of the State Legislature.

No Person shall be a Representative who shall not have attained the Age of twenty five Years, and been seven Years a Citizen of the United States, and who shall not, when elected, be an Inhabitant of that State in which he shall be chosen.

[Representatives and direct Taxes shall be apportioned among the several States which may be included within this Union, according to their respective Numbers, which shall be determined by adding to the whole Number of free Persons, including those bound to Service for a Term of Years, and excluding Indians not taxed, three fifths of all other Persons.][1] The actual Enumeration shall be made within three Years after the first Meeting of the Congress of the United States, and within every subsequent Term of ten Years, in such Manner as they shall by Law direct. The Number of Representatives shall not exceed *one for every thirty Thousand*, but each State shall have at Least one Representative; and until such enumeration shall be made, the State of New Hampshire shall be entitled to chuse three, Massachusetts eight, Rhode-Island and Providence Plantations one, Connecticut five, New-York six, New Jersey four, Pennsylvania eight, Delaware one, Maryland six, Virginia ten, North Carolina five, South Carolina five, and Georgia three.

When vacancies happen in the Representation from any State, the Executive Authority thereof shall issue Writs of Election to fill such Vacancies.

The House of Representatives shall chuse their Speaker and other Officers; and shall have the sole *Power of Impeachment.*

Section. 3. *The **Senate** of the United States shall be composed of two Senators from each State, [chosen by the Legislature][2] thereof for six Years; and each Senator shall have one Vote.

Immediately after they shall be assembled in Consequence of the first Election, they shall be divided as equally as may be into three Classes. The Seats of the Senators of the first Class shall be vacated at the Expiration of the second Year, of the second Class at the Expiration of the fourth Year, and of the third Class at the Expiration of the sixth Year, so that one third may be chosen every second Year; [and if Vacancies happen by Resignation, or otherwise, during Recess of the Legislature of any State, the Executive thereof may make temporary Appointments until the next Meeting of the Legislature, which shall then fill such Vacancies][3].

No Person shall be a Senator who shall not have attained to the Age of thirty Years, and been nine Years a Citizen of the United States, and who shall not, when elected, be an Inhabitant of that State for which he shall be chosen.

The Vice President of the United States shall be President of the Senate, but shall have no Vote, unless they be equally divided.

The Senate shall chuse their other Officers, and also a President pro tempore, in the Absence of the Vice President, or when he shall exercise the Office of President of the United States.

The Senate shall have the sole Power to *try all Impeachments*. When sitting for that Purpose, they shall be on Oath or Affirmation. When the President of the United States is tried, the Chief Justice shall preside: And no Person shall be convicted without the Concurrence of two thirds of the Members present.

Judgment in Cases of Impeachment shall not extend further than to removal from Office, and disqualification to hold and enjoy any Office of honor, Trust or Profit under the United States: but the Party convicted shall nevertheless be liable and subject to Indictment, Trial, Judgment and Punishment, according to Law.

Section. 4. The Times, Places and Manner of hold Elections for Senators and Representatives, shall be prescribed in each State by the Legislature thereof; but the Congress may at any time by law make or alter such Regulations, except as to the Places of chusing Senators.

The Congress shall assemble at least once in every Year, and such Meeting shall [be on the first Monday in December,][4] unless they shall by Law appoint a different Day.

Section. 5. Each House shall be the Judge of the Elections, Returns and Qualifications of its own Members, and a Majority of each shall constitute a Quorum to do Business; but a smaller Number may adjourn from day to day, and may be authorized to compel the Attendance of absent Members, in such Manner, and under such Penalties as each House may provide.

Each House shall keep a Journal of its Proceedings, and from time to time publish the same, excepting such Parts as may in their Judgment require Secrecy; and the Yeas and Nays of the Members of either House on any question shall, at the Desire of one fifth of those Present, be entered on the Journal.

Neither House, during the Session of Congress, shall, without the Consent of the other, adjourn for more than three days, nor to any other Place than that in which the two Houses shall be sitting.

Section. 6. The Senators and Representatives shall receive a Compensation for their Services, to be ascertained by law, and paid out of the Treasury of the United States. They shall in all Cases, except Treason, Felony and Breach of the Peace, be *privileged from Arrest* during their Attendance at the Session of their respective Houses, and in going to and returning from the same; and for any speech or Debate in either House, they shall not be questioned by any other Place.

No Senator or Representative shall, during the Time for which he was elected, be appointed to any civil Office under the Authority of the United States, which shall have been created, or the Emoluments whereof shall have been increased during such time; and no Person holding any Office under the United States, shall be a Member of either House during his Continuance in Office.

Section. 7. All Bills for *raising **Revenue*** shall originate *in the House of Representatives*; but the Senate may propose or concur with Amendments as on other Bills.

Every Bill which shall have passed the House of Representatives and the Senate, shall, before it become a

Law, be presented to the President of the United States: If he approve he shall sign it, but if not he shall return it, with his Objections to the House in which it shall have originated, who shall enter the Objections at large on their Journal, and proceed to reconsider it. If after such Reconsideration two thirds of that House shall agree to pass the Bill, it shall be sent, together with the Objections, to the other House, by which it shall likewise be reconsidered, and if approved by two thirds of that House, it shall become a Law. But in all such Cases the Votes of both Houses shall be determined by yeas and Nays, and the Names of the Persons voting for and against the Bill shall be entered on the Journal of each House respectively. If any Bill shall not be returned by the President within ten Days (Sundays excepted) after it shall have been presented to him, the Same shall be a Law, in like Manner as if he had signed it, unless the Congress by the Adjournment prevent its Return, in which Case it shall not be a Law.

Every Order, Resolution, or Vote to which the Concurrence of the Senate and House of Representatives may be necessary (except on a question of Adjournment) shall be presented to the President of the United States; and before the Same shall take Effect, shall be approved by him, or being disapproved by him, shall be repassed by two thirds of the Senate and House of Representatives, according to the Rules and Limitations prescribed in the Case of a Bill.

Section. 8. The Congress shall have Power To lay and collect *Taxes*, Duties, Imposts and *Excises*, to pay the Debts and provide for the common Defence and general Welfare of the United States; but all Duties, Imposts and Excises *shall be **uniform** throughout the United States;*

To borrow Money on the credit of the United States;

To regulate Commerce with foreign Nations, and among the several States, and with the Indian Tribes;

To establish an uniform *Rule of Naturalization*, and uniform Laws on the subject of Bankruptcies throughout the United States;

To *coin Money*, regulate the Value thereof, and of foreign Coin, and fix the Standard of Weights and Measures;

To provide for the Punishment of counterfeiting the Securities and current Coin of the United States;

To establish *Post Offices* and post Roads;

To promote the Progress of Science and useful Arts, by securing for limited Times to *Authors and Inventors* the exclusive Right to their respective Writings and Discoveries;

To constitute Tribunals inferior to the supreme Court;

To define and punish Piracies and Felonies committed on the high Seas, and Offences against the Law of Nations;

To **declare War**, grant Letters of Marque and Reprisal, and make Rules concerning Captures on Land and Water;

To raise and support Armies, but no Appropriation of Money to that use shall be for a longer Term than two years;

To provide and maintain a Navy;

To make Rules for the Government and Regulation of the land and naval Forces;

To provide for calling forth the Militia to execute the Laws of the Union, suppress Insurrections and repel Invasions;

To provide for organizing, arming, and disciplining, the *Militia*, and for governing such Part of them as may be employed in the Service of the United States, reserving to the States respectively, the Appointment of the Officers, and the Authority of training the Militia according to the discipline prescribed by Congress;

To exercise exclusive Legislation in all Cases whatsoever, over such District (not exceeding ten Miles square) as may, by Cession of particular States, and the Acceptance of Congress, become the Seat of the Government of the United States, and to exercise like Authority over all Places purchased by the Consent of the Legislature of the State in which the Same shall be, for the Erection of Forts, Magazines, Arsenals, dock-Yards, and other needful Buildings; – And

To make all Laws which shall be necessary and proper for carrying into Execution the foregoing Powers, and all other Powers vested by this Constitution in the Government of the United States, or in any Department or Officer thereof.

Section. 9. The Migration or Importation of such Persons as any of the States now existing shall think proper to admit, shall not be prohibited by the Congress prior to the Year one thousand eight hundred and eight, but a Tax or duty may be imposed on such Importation, not exceeding ten dollars for each Person.

The Privilege of the Writ of Habeas Corpus shall not be suspended, unless when in Cases of Rebellion or Invasion the public Safety may require it.

No Bill of Attainder or ***ex post facto*** *Law* shall be passed.

No Capitation, or other direct, Tax shall be laid, [unless in Proportion to the Census or enumeration herein before directed to be taken].[5]

No Tax or Duty shall be laid on *Articles exported from any State.*

No Preference shall be given by any Regulation of Commerce or Revenue to the Ports of *one State over those of another*; nor shall Vessels bound to, or from, one State, be obliged to enter, clear, or pay Duties in another.

No Money shall be drawn from the Treasury, but in Consequence of Appropriations made by law; and a regular Statement and Account of the Receipts and Expenditures of all public Money shall be published from time to time.

No Title of *Nobility* shall be granted by the United States: and no Person holding any Office of Profit or Trust under them, shall, without the Consent of the Congress, accept of any present, Emolument, Office, or Title, of any kind whatever, from any King, Prince, or foreign State.

Section. 10. *No State* shall enter into any *Treaty*, Alliance, or Confederation; grant Letters of Marque and Reprisal; coin Money; emit Bills of Credit; make any Thing but *gold and silver Coin* a Tender in Payment of Debts; pass any Bill of Attainder, ex post facto Law, or Law impairing the Obligation of Contracts, or grant any Title of Nobility.

No State shall, without the Consent of the Congress, lay any *Imposts* or Duties on Imports or Exports, except what may be absolutely necessary for executing its inspection Laws: and the net Produce of all Duties and Imposts, laid by any State on Imports or Exports, shall be for the Use of the Treasury of the United States; and all such Laws shall be subject to the Revision and Controul of the Congress.

No State shall, without the Consent of Congress, lay any Duty of Tonnage, keep Troops, or Ships of War in time of Peace, enter into any Agreement or Compact with another State, or with a foreign Power, or engage in War, unless actually invaded, or in such imminent Danger as will not admit of delay.

Article. II.

Section. 1. The *executive* Power shall be vested in a President of the United States of America. He shall hold his Office during the Term of four Years, and, together with the Vice President, chosen for the same Term, be elected, as follows:

Each State shall appoint, in such Manner as the Legislature thereof may direct, a Number of *Electors*, equal to the whole Number of Senators and Representatives to which the State may be entitled in the Congress: but no Senator or Representative, or Person holding an Office of Trust or Profit under the United States, shall be appointed an Elector.

[The Electors shall meet in their respective States, and vote by Ballot for two Persons, of whom one at least shall not be an Inhabitant of the same State with themselves. And they shall make a List of all the Persons voted for, and of the Number of Votes for each, which List they shall sign and certify, and transmit sealed to the Seat of the Government of the United States, *directed to the President* of the Senate. The President of the Senate shall, in the Presence of the Senate and House of Representatives, open all the Certificates, and the Votes shall then be counted. The Person having the *greatest Number of Votes shall be the President*, if such Number be a Majority of the whole Number of Electors appointed; and if there be more than one who have such Majority, and have an equal Number of Votes, then the House of Representatives shall immediately chuse by Ballot one of them for President; and if no Person have a Majority, then from the five highest on the List the said House shall in like Manner chuse the President. But in chusing the President, the Votes shall be taken by States, the Representation from each State having one Vote; A quorum for this purpose shall consist of a Member or Members from two thirds of the States, and a Majority of all the States shall be necessary to a Choice. In every Case, *after the Choice of the President, the Person having the greatest Number of Votes of the Electors shall be the Vice President.* But if there should remain two or more who have equal Vote, the Senate shall chuse from them by Ballot the Vice President.][6]

The Congress may determine the Time of chusing the Electors, and the Day on which they shall give their Votes; which Day shall be the same throughout the United States.

No Person except a natural born Citizen, or a Citizen of the United States, at the time of the Adoption of this Constitution, shall be eligible to the Office of President; neither shall any Person be eligible to that Office who shall not have attained to the Age of thirty five Years, and been fourteen Years a Resident within the United States.

[In Case of the *Removal of the President* from Office, or of his Death, Resignation, or Inability to discharge the Powers and Duties of the said Office, the Same shall devolve on the Vice president, and the Congress may by law provide for the Case of Removal, Death, Resignation or Inability, both of the President and Vice President, declaring what Officer shall then act as President, and such Officer shall act accordingly, until the Disability be removed, or a President shall be elected.][7]

The President shall, at stated Times, receive for his Services, a Compensation, which shall neither be increased nor diminished during the Period for which he shall have been elected, and he shall not receive within that Period any other Emolument from the United States, or any of them.

Before he enter on the Execution of his Office, he shall take the following *Oath* or Affirmation: – "I do solemnly swear (or affirm) that I will faithfully execute the Office of President of the United States, and will to the best of my Ability, *preserve, protect and defend the Constitution* of the United States."

Section. 2. The President shall be **Commander in Chief** of the Army and Navy of the United States, and of the Militia of the several States, when called into the actual Service of the United States; he may require the Opinion, in writing, of the principal Office in each of the executive Departments upon any Subject relating to the Duties of their respective Offices, and he shall have Power to grant Reprieves and Pardons for Offences against the United States, except in Cases of Impeachment.

He shall have Power, by and **with the Advice and Consent of the Senate**, to make Treaties provided two thirds of the Senators present concur, and he shall nominate, and by and with the Advice and Consent of the Senate, shall appoint Ambassadors, other public ministers and Consuls, Judges of the supreme court, and all other Officers of the United States, whose Appointments are not herein otherwise provided for, and which shall be established by Law: but the Congress may by Law vest the Appointment of such inferior Officers, as they think proper, in the President alone, in the Courts of Law; or in the Heads of Departments.

The President shall have Power to fill up all *Vacancies* that may happen *during the Recess of the Senate*, by granting Commissions which shall expire at the End of their next *Session*.

Section. 3. He shall from time to time give to the Congress Information of the State of the Union, and recommend to their Consideration such Measures as he shall judge necessary and expedient; he may, on extraordinary Occasions, convene both Houses, or either of them, and in Case of Disagreement between them, with Respect to the Time of Adjournment, he may adjourn them to such Time as he shall think proper; he shall receive Ambassadors and other public ministers; ***he shall take Care that the Laws be faithfully executed***, and shall Commission all the Officers of the United States.

Section. 4. The president, Vice President and all civil Officers of the United States, shall be removed from Office on impeachment for, and Conviction of, Treason, Bribery, or other high Crimes and Misdemeanors.

Article III.

Section. 1. The *judicial* Power of the United States shall be vested in one supreme Court, and in such inferior Courts as the Congress may from time to time ordain and establish. The Judges, both of the supreme and inferior Courts, shall hold their Offices *during good Behaviour*, and shall, at stated Times, receive for their Services a Compensation, which shall not be diminished during their Continuance in Office.

Section. 2. The judicial Power shall extend to all Cases, in Law and Equity, arising under this Constitution, the Laws of the United States, and Treaties made, or which shall be made, under their Authority; – to All Cases affecting Ambassadors, other public Ministers and Consuls; – to all Cases of admiralty and maritime Jurisdiction; – to Controversies to which the United States shall be a Party; – to Controversies between two or more States; – [between a State and Citizens of another State;][8] – *between Citizens of different States*; – between Citizens of the same State claiming Lands under Grants of different States, [and between a State, or the Citizens thereof, and foreign States, Citizens or Subjects.][9]

In all Cases affecting Ambassadors, other public Ministers and Consuls, and those in which a State shall be Party, the supreme Court shall have original Jurisdiction. In all the other Cases before mentioned, the supreme Court shall have appellate Jurisdiction, both as to Law and Fact, with such Exceptions, and under such Regulations as the Congress shall make.

The Trial of all Crimes, except in Cases of Impeachment, shall be by Jury; and such Trial shall be held in the State where the said Crimes shall have been committed; but when not committed within any State, the Trial shall be at such Place or Places as the Congress may by Law have directed.

Section. 3. *Treason* against the United States, shall consist only in levying War against them, or in adhering to their Enemies, giving them Aid and Comfort. No Person shall be convicted of Treason unless on the Testimony of two Witnesses to the same overt Act, or in Confession in open court.

The Congress shall have Power to declare the Punishment of Treason, but no Attainder of Treason shall work Corruption of Blood, or Forfeiture except during the Life of the Person attainted.

Article. IV.

Section. 1. Full Faith and Credit shall be given in each State to the public Acts, Records, and judicial Proceedings of every other State. And the congress may by general Laws prescribe the Manner in which such Acts, Records and Proceedings shall be proved, and the Effect thereof.

Section. 2. *The* **Citizens of each State shall be entitled to all Privileges and Immunities of Citizens in the several States.**

A Person charged in any State with Treason, Felony, or other Crime, who shall fell from Justice, and be found in another State, shall on Demand of the executive Authority of the State from which he fled, be delivered up, to be removed to the State having Jurisdiction of the Crime.

[No Person held to Service or Labour in one State, under the Laws thereof, escaping into another, shall, in Consequence of any Law or Regulation therein, be discharged from such Service or Labour, but shall be delivered up on Claim o fhte Party to whom such Service or Labour may be due.][10]

Section. 3. New States may be admitted by the Congress into this Union; but no new State shall be formed or erected within the Jurisdiction of any other State; nor any State be formed by the Junction of two or more States, or Parts of States, without the Consent of the Legislatures of the States concerned as well as of the Congress.

The Congress shall have Power to dispose of and make all needful Rules and Regulations respecting the Territory or other Property belonging to the United States; and nothing in this Constitution shall be so construed as to Prejudice any Claims of the United States, or of *any particular State.*

Section. 4. The United States shall guarantee to every State in this Union a ***Republican*** form of Government, and shall protect each of them against Invasion;

and on Application of the Legislature, or of the Executive (when the Legislature cannot be convened), against domestic Violence.

Article. V.

The Congress, whenever two thirds of both Houses shall deem it necessary, shall propose **Amendments** to this Constitution, or, on the Application of the Legislatures of two thirds of the several States, shall call a Convention for proposing Amendments, which, in either Case, shall be valid to all Intents and Purposes, as Part of this Constitution, when ratified by the Legislatures of three fourths of the several States or by Conventions in three fourths thereof, as the one or the other Mode of ratification may be proposed by the Congress; Provided that no Amendment which may be made prior to the Year One thousand eight hundred and eight shall in any Manner affect the first and fourth Clauses in the Ninth Section of the first Article; and that no State, without its Consent, shall be deprived of its equal Suffrage in the Senate.

Article. VI.

All Debts contracted and Engagements entered into, before the Adoption of this Constitution, shall be as valid against the United States under this Constitution, as under the Confederation.

This Constitution, and the Laws of the United States which shall be made in Pursuance thereof; and all Treaties made, or which shall be made, under the Authority of the United States, shall be the supreme Law of the Land; and the Judges in every State shall be bound thereby, any

Thing in the Constitution or Laws of any State to the Contrary notwithstanding.

The Senators and Representatives before mentioned, and the Members of the several State Legislatures, and all executive and judicial Officers, both of the United States and of the several States, shall be bound by *Oath or Affirmation, to support this Constitution, but* **no religious Test** *shall ever be required* as a Qualification to any Office or public Trust under the United States.

Article. VII.

The Ratification of the conventions of nine States, shall be sufficient for the Establishment of this Constitution between the States so ratifying the Same.

Done in convention by the Unanimous Consent of the States present the Seventeenth Day of September in the Year of our Lord one thousand seven hundred and Eighty seven and of the Independence of the United States of America the Twelfth In witness whereof We have hereunto subscribed our Names,

Go. Washington
Presidt and deputy from Virginia

Delaware

Geo: Read
Gunning Bedford jun
John Dickinson
Richard Bassett
Jaco: Broom

Maryland

James McHenry
Dan of St Thos. Jenifer
Danl. Carroll

Virginia	John Blair
	James Madison Jr.
North Carolina	Wm. Blount
	Richd. Dobbs Spaight
	Hu Williamson
South Carolina	J. Rutledge
	Charles Cotesworth Pinckney
	Charles Pinckney
	Pierce Butler
Georgia	William Few
	Abr Baldwin
New Hampshire	John Langdon
	Nicholas Gilman
Massachusetts	Nathaniel Gorham
	Rufus King
Connecticut	Wm. Saml. Johnson
	Roger Sherman
New York	Alexander Hamilton
New Jersey	Wil: Livingston
	David Brearley
	Wm. Paterson
	Jona: Dayton
Pennsylvania	B Franklin
	Thomas Mifflin
	Robt. Morris
	Geo. Clymer

Thos. FitzSimons
Jared Ingersoll
James Wilson
Gouv Morris

Attest   William   Jackson
Secretary

Notes:

[1] Changed by Section 2 of the Fourteenth Amendment.
[2] Changed by the Seventeenth Amendment.
[3] Changed by the Seventeenth Amendment.
[4] Changed by section 2 of the Twentieth Amendment.
[5] See Sixteenth Amendment.
[6] Changed by the Twelfth Amendment.
[7] Changed by the Twenty-Fifth Amendment.
[8] Changed by the Eleventh Amendment.
[9] Changed by the Thirteenth Amendment.

AMENDMENTS TO THE CONSTITUTION OF THE UNITED STATES

Amendment I[1]

Congress shall make no law respecting an establishment of *religion*, or prohibiting the free exercise thereof; or abridging the freedom of *speech*, or of the *press*; or the right of the people peaceable to assemble, and to petition the Government for a redress of grievances.

Amendment II

A well regulated Militia, being necessary to the security of a free Stte, the right of the people to keep and bear *Arms,* shall not be infringed.

Amendment III

No Soldier shall, in time of peace be quartered in any house without the consent of the Owner, nor in time of war, but in a manner to be prescribed by law.

Amendment IV

The right of the people to be secure in their persons, houses, papers, and effects, against *unreasonable searches* and seizures, shall not be violated, and no Warrants shall issue, but upon *probably cause*, supported by Oath or affirmation, and particularly describing the place to be searched, and the persons or things to be seized.

Amendment V

No person shall be held to answer for a capital, or otherwise infamous crime, unless on a presentment or indictment of a Grand Jury, except in cases arising in the land or naval forces, or in the Militia, when in actual service in time of War or public danger; nor shall any person be subject for the same offence to be *twice* put in jeopardy of life or limb; nor shall be compelled in any criminal case to be a *witness against himself*, nor be deprived of life, liberty, or property, without due process of law; nor shall private property be taken for public use, without just compensation.

Amendment VI

In all criminal prosecutions, the accused shall enjoy the right to a *speedy and public trial*, by an impartial jury of the State and district wherein the crime shall have been committed, which district shall have been previously ascertained by law, and to be informed of the nature and cause of the accusation; to be confronted with the witnesses against him; to have compulsory process for obtaining witnesses in his favor, and to have the Assistance of *Counsel* for his defence.

Amendment VII

In Suits at common law, where the value in controversy shall exceed twenty dollars, the right of *trial by jury* shall be preserved, and no fact tried by a jury, shall be otherwise re-examined in any court of the United States, than according to the rules of the common law.

Amendment VIII

Excessive *bail* shall not be required, nor *excessive fines* imposed, nor cruel and unusual punishments inflicted.

Amendment IX

The *enumeration* in the Constitution, of certain rights, shall not be construed to deny or disparage others retained by the people.

Amendment X

The *powers not delegated to the United States by the Constitution*, nor prohibited by it to the States, are *reserved to the States* respectively, or to the people.

Amendment XI[2]

The Judicial power of the United States shall not be construed to extend to any suit in law or equity, commenced or prosecuted against one of the United States by Citizens of another State, or by Citizens or Subjects of any Foreign State.

Amendment XII[3]

The *Electors shall meet in their respective states* and vote by ballot for president and Vice-President, one of whom, at least, shall not be an inhabitant of the same state with themselves; they shall name in their ballots the person voted for as President, and in *distinct ballots* the person voted for as *Vice-President*, and they shall make distinct lists of all persons voted for as President, and of all persons voted for as Vice-President, and of the number of votes for each, which lists they shall sign and certify, and transmit sealed to the seat of the government of the United States, directed to the President of the Senate; – the President of the Senate shall, in the presence of the Senate and House of Representatives, open all the certificates and the votes shall then be counted; – The person having the greatest number of votes for President, shall be the President, if such number be a majority of the whole number of Electors appointed; and if no person have such majority, then from the persons having the highest numbers not exceeding three on the list of those voted for as President, the House of Representatives shall choose immediately, by ballot, the President. But in choosing the President, the votes shall be taken by states, the representation from each state having one vote; a quorum for this purpose shall consist of a member or members from two-thirds of the states, and a majority of all the states shall be necessary to a choice. [And if the House of Representatives shall not choose a President whenever the right of choice shall devolve upon them, before the fourth day of March next following, then the Vice-President shall act as President, as in case of the death or other constitutional disability of the President. —][4] The person having the greatest number of votes as Vice-President, shall be the Vice-President, if such number be a majority of the whole number of Electors appointed, and if no person have a majority, then from the two highest numbers on the list, the Senate shall choose the Vice-President; a quorum for the purpose shall consist of two-thirds of the whole number of Senators, and a majority of the whole number shall be necessary to a choice. But no person constitutionally ineligible to the office of President shall be eligible to that of Vice-President of the United States.

Amendment XIII[5]

Section 1. Neither *slavery* nor involuntary servitude, except as a punishment for crime whereof the party shall have been duly convicted, shall exist within the United States, or any place subject to their jurisdiction.

Section 2. Congress shall have power to enforce this article by appropriate legislation.

Amendment XIV[6]

Section 1. All persons born or naturalized in the United States, and subject to the jurisdiction thereof, are citizens of the United States and of the State wherein they reside. No State shall make or enforce any law which shall abridge the privileges or immunities of citizens of the United States; nor shall any State deprive any person of life, liberty, or property, without due process of law; nor deny to any person within its jurisdiction the *equal protection* of the laws.

Section 2. Representatives shall be apportioned among the several States according to their respective numbers, counting the whole number of persons in each State, *excluding Indians not taxed.* But when the right to vote at any election for the choice of electors for President and Vice-President of the United States, Representatives in Congress, the Executive and Judicial officers of a State, or the members of the Legislature thereof, is denied to any of the *male* inhabitants of such State, being twenty-one years of age, and citizens of the United States, or in any way abridged, except for participation in rebellion, or other crime, the basis of representation therein shall be reduced in the proportion which the number of such male citizens shall bear to the whole number of male citizens twenty-one years of age in such State.

Section 3. No person shall be a Senator or Representative in Congress, or elector of President and Vice-President, or hold any office, civil or military, under the United States, or under any State, who having previously taken an oath, as a member of Congress, or as an officer of the United States, or as a member of any State legislature, or as an executive or judicial officer of any State, to support the Constitution of the United States, shall have engaged in insurrection or rebellion against the same, or given aid or comfort to the enemies thereof. But congress may by a vote of two-thirds of each House, remove such disability.

Section 4. The validity of the public debt of the United States, authorized by law, including debts incurred for payment of pensions and bounties for services in suppressing insurrection or rebellion shall not be questioned. But neither the United States nor any State shall assume or pay any debt or obligation incurred in aid of insurrection or rebellion against the United States, or any claim for the loss or emancipation of any slave; but all such debts, obligations and claims shall be held illegal and void.

Section 5. The Congress shall have the power to enforce, by appropriate legislation, the provisions of this article.

Amendment XV[7]

Section 1. The right of citizens of the United States to vote shall not be denied or abridged by the United States or by any State on account of *race,* color, or previous condition of servitude –

Section 2. The Congress shall have the power to enforce this article by appropriate legislation.

Amendment XVI[8]

The Congress shall have power to lay and collect *taxes on incomes,* from whatever source derived, without apportionment among the several States, and without regard to any census or enumeration.

Amendment XVII[9]

The *Senate* of the United States shall be composed of *two* Senators from each State, elected by the people thereof, for six years; and each Senator shall have one vote. The electors in each State shall have the qualifications requisite for electors of the most numerous branch of the State legislatures.

When vacancies happen in the representation of any State in the Senate, the executive authority of such State shall issue writs of election to fill such vacancies:

Provided, That the legislature of any State may empower the executive thereof to make temporary appointments until the people fill the vacancies by election as the legislature may direct.

This amendment shall not be so construed as to affect the election or term of any Senator chosen before it becomes valid as part of the Constitution.

Amendment XVIII[10]

Section 1. After one year from the ratification of this article the manufacture, sale, or transportation of intoxicating *liquors* within, the importation thereof into, or the exportation thereof from the United States and all territory subject to the jurisdiction thereof for beverage purposes is hereby prohibited.

Section 2. The Congress and the several States shall have concurrent power to enforce this article by appropriate legislation.

Section 3. This article shall be inoperative unless it shall have been ratified as an amendment to the Constitution by the legislatures of the several States, as provided in the Constitution, within seven years from the date of the submission hereof to the States by the Congress.

Amendment XIX[11]

The right of citizens of the United States to vote shall not be denied or abridged by the United States or by any State on account of *sex*.

Congress shall have power to enforce this article by appropriate legislation.

Amendment XX[12]

Section 1. The terms of the President and the Vice President shall end at noon on the 20th day of January, and the terms of Senators and Representatives at noon on the 3d day of January, of the years in which such terms would have ended if this article had not been ratified; and the terms of their successors shall then begin.

Section 2. The Congress shall assemble at least once in every year, and such meeting shall begin at noon on the 3d day of January, unless they shall by law appoint a different day.

Section 3. If, at the time fixed for the beginning of the term of the President, the President elect shall have died, the Vice President elect shall become President. If a President shall not have been chosen before the time fixed for the beginning of his term, or if the President elect shall have failed to qualify, then the Vice President elect shall act as President until a President shall have qualified; and the Congress may by law provide for the case wherein neither a President elect nor a Vice President shall have qualified, declaring who shall then act as President, or the manner in which one who is to act shall be selected, and such person shall act accordingly until a President or Vice President shall have qualified.

Section 4. The Congress may by law provide for the case of the death of any of the persons from whom the House of Representatives may choose a President whenever the right of choice shall have devolved upon them, and for the case of the death of any of the persons from whom the senate may choose a Vice President whenever the right of choice shall have devolved upon them.

Section 5. Sections 1 and 2 shall take effect on the 15th day of October following the ratification of this article.

Section 6. This article shall be inoperative unless it shall have been ratified as an amendment to the Constitution by the legislatures of three-fourths of the several States within seven years from the date of its submission.

Amendment XXI[13]

Section 1. The eighteenth article of amendment to the Constitution of the United States is hereby repealed.

Section 2. The transportation or importation into any State, Territory, or Possession of the United States for delivery or use therein of intoxicating *liquors,* violation of the laws thereof, is hereby prohibited.

Section 3. This article shall be inoperative unless it shall have been ratified as an amendment to the Constitution by conventions in the several States as provided in the Constitution, within seven years from the date of the submission hereof to the States by the Congress.

Amendment XXII[14]

Section 1. No person shall be elected to the office of the President *more than twice,* and no person who has held the office of President, or acted as President, for more than two years of a term to which some other person was elected President shall be elected to the office of President more than once. But this Article shall not apply to any person holding the office of President when this Article was proposed by congress, and shall not prevent any person who may be holding the office of President, or acting as President, during the term within which this Article becomes operative from holding the office of President or acting as President during the remainder of such term.

Section 2. This article shall be inoperative unless it shall have been ratified as an amendment to the Constitution by the legislatures of three-fourths of the several

States within seven years from the date of its submission to the States by the Congress.

Amendment XXIII[15]

Section 1. *The District* constituting the seat of Government of the United States shall appoint in such manner as Congress may direct:

A number of electors of President and Vice President equal to the whole number of Senators and Representatives in Congress to which the District would be entitles if it were a State, but in no event more than the least populous State; they shall be in addition to those appointed by the States, but they shall be considered, for the purposes of the election of President and Vice President, to be electors appointed by a State, and they shall meet in the District and perform such duties as provided by the twelfth article of amendment.

Section 2. The Congress shall have power to enforce this article by appropriate legislation.

Amendment XXIV[16]

Section 1. The right of citizens of the United States to vote in any primary or other election for President or Vice President, for electors for President or Vice President, or for Senator or Representative in Congress, shall not be denied or abridged by the United States or any State by reason of failure to pay *poll tax* or other tax.

Section 2. The Congress shall have power to enforce this article by appropriate legislation.

Amendment XXV[17]

Section 1. In case of the *removal of the President* from office or of his death or resignation, the Vice President shall become President.

Section 2. Whenever there is a vacancy in the office of the Vice president, the President shall nominate a Vice President who shall take office upon confirmation by a majority vote of both Houses of Congress.

Section 3. Whenever the President transmits to the President pro tempore of the Senate and the Speaker of the House of Representatives hiw written declaration that he is unable to discharge the powers and duties of his office, and until he transmits to them a written declaration to the contrary, such powers and duties shall be discharged by the Vice President as Acting president.

Section 4. Whenever the Vice President and a majority of either the principal officers of the executive departments or of such other body as Congress may by law provide, transmit to the President pro tempore of the Senate and the Speaker of the House of representatives their written declaration that the President is unable to discharge the powers and duties of his office, the Vice President shall immediately assume the powers and duties of the office as Acting President.

Thereafter, when the President transmits to the President pro tempore of the Senate and the Speaker of the House of Representatives his written declaration that no inability exists, he shall resume the powers and duties of his office unless the Vice President and a majority of either the principal officers of the executive department or of such other body as Congress may by law provide, transmit within four days to the President pro tempore of the Senate and the Speaker of the House of representatives their written declaration that the President is unable to discharge the powers and duties of his office. Thereupon Congress shall decide the issue, assembling within forty-eight hours for that purpose if not in session. If the Congress, within twenty-one days after receipt of the latter written declaration, or, if Congress is not in session, within twenty-one days after Congress is required to assemble, determines by two-thirds vote of both Houses that the President is unable to discharge the powers and duties of his office, the Vice President shall continue to discharge the same as Acting President; otherwise the President shall resume the powers and duties of his office.

Amendment XXVI[18]

Section 1. The right of citizens of the United States, who are *eighteen years of age* or older, to vote shall not be denied or abridged by the United States or by any State on account of age.

Section 2. the Congress shall have power to enforce this article by appropriate legislation.

Amendment XXVII[19]

No law, varying the *compensation* for the services of the Senators and Representatives, shall take effect, until an election of representatives shall have intervened.

Notes:

1. The first ten Amendments (Bill of Rights) were ratified effective December 15, 1791.
2. The Eleventh Amendment was ratified February 7, 1795.
3. The Twelfth Amendment was ratified June 15, 1804.
4. Superseded by section 3 of the Twentieth Amendment.
5. The Thirteenth Amendment was ratified December 6, 1865.

6   The fourteenth Amendment was ratified July 9, 1868.

7   The Fifteenth Amendment was ratified February 3, 1870.

8   The Sixteenth Amendment was ratified February 3, 1913.

9   The Seventeenth Amendment was ratified April 8, 1913.

10 The Eighteenth Amendment was ratified January 16, 1919. It was repealed by the Twenty-First Amendment December 5, 1933.

11 The nineteenth Amendment was ratified August 18, 1920.

12 The Twentieth Amendment was ratified January 23, 1933.

13 The Twenty-First Amendment was ratified December 5, 1933.

14 The Twenty-Second Amendment was ratified February 27, 1951.

15 The Twenty-Third Amendment was ratified March 29, 1961.

16 The Twenty-Fourth Amendment was ratified January 23, 1964.

17 The Twenty-Fifth Amendment was ratified February 10, 1967.

18 The Twenty-Sixth Amendment was ratified July 1, 1971.

19 The Twenty-Seventh Amendment was ratified May 7, 1992.

EPILOGUE

I feel I have done my duty. I used to work for IBM, when I worked there the motto printed on many items was "THINK." Management felt that a secret of their success was that they encouraged their people to think. My purpose in writing this book is to try to encourage people to think; to decide what they believe.

I had to stop at some point even though the Media keeps adding material for the book. The way the media tries to influence what we think by the way they report events. The emphasis they place on safety sensationalizes air controller's that sleep on the job and "near" mid-air collisions. We get reports of congressional debates over the budget while it appears that most Congressmen are unconcerned about the Survival of America. With reports of world conflicts, we are left wondering what we will do next.

Had I had more time, I would have added new chapters to reflect my thoughts in different areas. These chapters might be; Customer Service, The Effect of the Legal Profession, The Election Process, The Melting Pot and Multi-lingualism. I will include these chapters in my second edition if it happens but you can probably guess what I will say.

Government *is* the problem; we must create the real vision of America.

I pray for America's survival.

ABOUT THE AUTHOR:

Hank Sims was born and raised on a farm in Missouri. He was educated his first eight years in a one-room school in Trimble. He has a Bachelor's and a Master's degree in Engineering. He hated history in high school and only became fascinated with it later. Along with histories of the Civil War and WWII he has read numerous historical books and biographies. A major reading was Volumes 1 through 8 of Will Durant's THE STORY OF CIVILIZATION.

The author likes potatoes. He likes peeled potatoes; mashed, fried, boiled or in casseroles. He learned that studies have shown that substantial vitamins are in the peels. He learned to accept his potatoes not peeled. Then he heard that it had been determined that pesticides and fertilizers permeated potato peels, thus the peels were unhealthy. Next, he learned that potato peels were healthy unless you could see obvious discoloration.

He began to wonder about the credentials of those advising him. He began to wonder who it was that he could believe.

In researching for this book, he became aware of how out of touch with America that he was. He was un-aware of the high unemployment in the early 1980's because he was employed. He didn't realize the meaning behind Newt Gingrich's "Contract with America" because he was too busy.

He only recently came to the conclusion that his support for the Iraq War was support for the troops, not the Mission.

His objective with this book is to portray what he believes to be true and encourage others to be aware, to see the world as it is, and to have some humility as they determine what they really believe, so they will act for what is right.